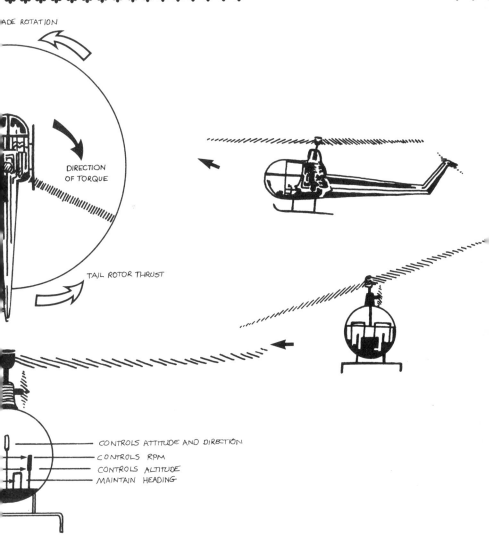

ADE ROTATION

DIRECTION
OF TORQUE

TAIL ROTOR THRUST

CONTROLS ATTITUDE AND DIRECTION
CONTROLS RPM
CONTROLS ALTITUDE
MAINTAIN HEADING

# VERTICAL ASCENT

## ADVENTURES OF A HELICOPTER PILOT

# Charles O. Weir

hancock

house

Copyright © 1977 **Charles O. Weir**
ISBN0-919654-76-2

*Cataloging in Publication Data*

Weir, Charles O.
    Vertical ascent.
    ISBN 0-919654-76-2

        1. Weir, Charles O. 2. Helicopters -
Piloting. 3. Air pilots - Biography.
I. Taylor, Leonard. II. Title.


    T.540.W38A38 1977        77.3516
        LCC 77-3516

PRINTED IN CANADA

Published by:

**Hancock House Publishers Ltd.**
3215 Island View Road
SAANICHTON, B.C. V0S 1M0

**Hancock House Publishers Inc.**
12008 1st Avenue South
SEATTLE, WA. 98168

# Contents

# Introduction

The helicopter has come a long way over the past three decades and even the people who have been directly involved with its design, manufacture and operations are impressed with the many achievements they have witnessed. Spanning the period from the early attempts at vertical flight to the sophisticated turbocopters of today, it is obvious that progress has been limited only by the imagination of the people involved.

The thousands of rescue operations performed by the helicopter have highlighted the public awareness of its tremendous versatility. It becomes obvious that the pattern is set for the future and the helicopter as a mode of transportation will become as much a part of our way of life as the train, bus or airplane. Somewhere at this moment there are helicopters being flown to offshore locations with crews and equipment; others are being flown on a variety of lift missions in construction work or flown as cranes for logging. Helicopters are regularly used to transport men and equipment to remote mountain – top sites for survey operations. They are called upon to aid in putting out forest fires. In addition, helicopters patrol power and pipelines and fly on avalanche control missions.

The face the public sees most frequently is that of the helicopter pilot and this story is about the experiences of one such man, Charles Weir. Charles, in relating his sixteen years flying experience, tells not only his own personal story, but the story of other veteran helicopter pilots as well – whose careers, in many instances, run parallel to his own.

**Vertical Ascent** will prove informative reading for any – one with a desire to learn a little more about the versatility of the helicopter and the remarkable people who fly them.

Alf Stringer, President
Vancouver Island Helicopters

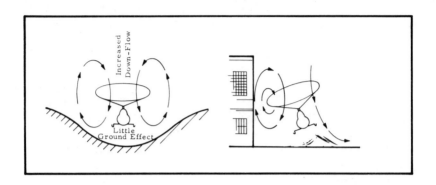

# 1

# Rough Landing

The valley was small, but from 4,000 feet up in the crisp Yukon air it appeared wide and smooth enough to form the landing pad I was seeking for my Bell 47-G2 helicopter. The open area was in the heart of the region in which I sought to land my passenger Bill Brisbin, chief of our exploration team, and he indicated he was satisfied with it. Brisbin, a University of Manitoba professor, was spending the summer of 1958 as a consultant to the California Standard Oil Co., which had its Canadian headquarters in Calgary. He was a veteran of these exploration trips but it was my first field assignment since becoming a pilot for Okanagan Helicopters Ltd., of Vancouver, B.C.

We expected a smooth easy descent, as flying conditions were perfect on that sparkling morning of June 12. Not that this would catch me off guard. Thousands of hours as a pilot of fixed-wing aircraft had impressed me with a deep respect for air safety rules and practices. I was acutely aware of the need for care. Strapped onto both side carriers of the copter were square tins of extra gasoline, 40 gallons in all, a considerable addition to the normal capacity of 600 pounds made up of two adults, supplies, emergency kit and the regular fuel supply.

I had started my summer's work at Summit Lake, the highest point on the Alaska Highway, a few weeks earlier, working out of a base camp at the 4000 foot level. Our main camp was established on the shore of lovely, tiny Syd Lake about 125 miles northeast of Dawson City, close to the Peel River. It was a good sheltered spot for 'copters and the lake offered a runway for float planes provided it was treated with respect, for it was barely long enough to accommodate takeoffs or landings.

We had scouted several possible landing sites that morning as we skimmed along, over and between ridges that ran up to 7000 feet, but none had met the double requisite of a safe landing and a safe liftoff, the latter the far more difficult part of the flying task in helicopters. I was cautious, for I was a rookie whirlybird pilot and well aware that nothing I had learned in 2500 hours of Royal Canadian Air Force flying service would be of specific use here.

The machine I was flying was no toy, but a sophisticated assembly of engineering genius, worth at least $50,000. As we corkscrewed our way down I got the uncomfortable feeling that what had appeared smooth at 4000 feet was, in fact, anything but that. A dip down to 100 feet showed that the area was studded with large boulders, some six or seven feet tall.We hovered above the ground, and I did a visual search upstream and down for a better spot, skittering down to a few feet from the ground in several places. As we dipped to inspect one possible area it happened: suddenly and unexpectedly.

The right rear tip of the aluminum alloy skid fixed under the 'copter jarred against a rock. The machine tipped dangerously, tail down, and I hurriedly 'poured on the coal' as 'copter pilots say when they shove their machines into full throttle. Getting down is easier than getting up, and although the engine roared we rose very slowly and it was obvious we had to get out of there as quickly as possible. Searching for the easiest escape route I opted for the valley of the stream, moving the 'copter uphill into a rising draft of air I felt would give extra lift. Technically, the idea was correct but geography appeared ignorant of flying theories for the stream narrowed rapidly and the fringe of trees on both banks moved in ominously.

I now realize I could have done things differently. The best

10

prospect would have been a smart about-turn and a dash downstream, regardless of the fact that we would be flying downwind on that course.

It was a grim struggle but we never really had a chance. With a mighty crash the 35-foot main rotor blades sheared the top off a tree on one side of the watercourse, lurched across and struck another on the opposite bank. We thrashed along, hitting tree tops in a zigzag pattern, each collision slowing the rotor and reducing the lift. Like a drunk in slow motion the 'copter staggered to earth, coming to rest near the bank of the stream.

Shaken, I climbed out—and then I really began to sweat. We had landed a foot from the edge of the bank, the starboard skid parallel to the edge, below which there was a 10-foot drop to the dry stream bed. Had we toppled into the watercourse the crash would have turned the machine on its side and without question would have spilled enough petrol to incinerate both of us.

Reaction to danger past can do strange things to you. It may make you giggle. It can make you cry. It can stun you into prolonged silence. I began to laugh. It struck me, all of a sudden, that the procedural rules require that a pilot enter in his log book the actual time that he lands. My flight would be hard to log, I thought. The machine had bounced on landing so often that I wasn't sure when I could say the flight ended—on the first bounce or the last. But I was thankful I would be able to make that entry personally and in one piece.

We were down in a trackless wilderness, 20 flying minutes from our base camp but God knows how many miles on the ground where one must climb over or walk around the mountains. Another nasty shock was the sudden realization that I had told no one at base where we intended to go when we took off. I had, in fact, not filed a flight plan. This essential information includes: course to be flown, distance, time in the air, fuel on board and number of persons on board. No one knew where we were and, because we were not expected to return until evening, no hunt for us could begin for half a day. It was the sin of the amateur, an omission which I had never been guilty of before and would never be again.

11

We had moved into Syd Lake late in May, a party of seven geologists, a cook and his helper, my engineer Bert Fallman, and me. I flew the helicopter in from Dawson but our main link to the outside world, that old mining community represented, was a Beaver float plane piloted by Bill Simpson, a skilled pilot who amazed us with the slick way in which he handled the limited water runway of Syd Lake.

I had been up about 5 a.m. that morning, checking the weather. We had no daily weather reports and I had to use my knowledge of the elements to make my own meteorological decisions. Brisbin appeared a few minutes after I had communed with the winds and the skies and I was able to assure him it would be a good working day. He gave me a general outline of the work plan which required me to drop off six geologists in pairs within a 25-mile radius of camp, then to pick him up and fly him to several points he would select. We were the only people who knew where all the parties would be and in our haste to get airborne we neglected to give the same plan to those who would remain at base.

The first three trips were uneventful. It was relaxed, enjoyable flying with all three pairs. We laughed and chatted, setting rendezvous times for pickups and my passengers soon disappeared into the bush.

Exploration parties prefer to travel in pairs for this was, and remains, truly wilderness country, abounding in wild life—wolves, grizzly bears, moose, among others.

There are no trails. Travel is hard and can be dangerous and the prospect of injury in bush and rock mountain country likely enough to make the use of the 'buddy' system both logical and necessary. The explorers carried food, matches in sealed containers, and each pair had one magnum revolver with enough hitting power to fend off bears.

After talking with Bill in the early morning I had realized I would need extra fuel so I had Fallman prepare the additional gasoline, securing it in even ranks of five-gallon tins on the carriers on the outside of the 'copter.

This particular machine used 14 gallons of fuel per hour in normal conditions, something I had to know as helicopter pilots seldom rely on fuel tank registration. They know their craft's consumption capacity, for testing has given them an accurate idea of the amount needed for an hour's flight. When in doubt I used a measuring dip stick in the tanks and copter pilots still take the same elementary precautions even in these days of jet engines and different types of fuel.

When we took off Bill and I were equipped with enough fuel for 350 miles of flight, so we could have crashed anywhere within a radius of 175 miles, the only fact that Fallman and the cook at base could possibly compute.

An added anxiety was the knowledge that the location of the three pairs set down before I picked up Bill was totally unknown to anyone but us. They were, although they could not yet know it, in the same danger of being castaways as we were.

Bill, an experienced woodsman, was sure we could walk out in a day or two just using a compass. We knew that a large, fast-moving river lay between us and our camp and that we had no way of crossing it, a fact that secretly pleased me, for I believe strongly that passengers and pilots are better off to stick with downed aircraft, something easier for rescuers to locate than a couple of people moving through bush country.

A signal fire was a clear necessity so we hauled dried branches and limbs of fallen trees to a spot in the open and piled them in a heap. Fires are hard to see in the daytime and in June in the Yukon there is no night: you can read a newspaper at two o'clock in the morning. I drained the oil from the helicopter and put it near the signal fire. It would make a nice black smoke if a rescue craft approached.

An inventory of our supplies showed we had a couple of sandwiches, three red flares, some tools, two rifles, a small stock of dehydrated food, fish hooks and a fish line. We need not starve even if our rescue was delayed.

The damaged 'copter was still in the open but close to the trees where shadows might make it difficult to spot from the air, and our lame duck obviously was well grounded until parts could be obtained. The main rotor blades, of laminated wood with a steel leading edge, were bent and split at the ends. Equally serious was the tail rotor: twisted and pointing off at a tangent, the result of it hitting a small tree as we had crashed. One skid was badly bent from the initial impact.

The main rotor is a delicate invention. The blades are so finely balanced in a well-tuned machine that in a hangar, under windless conditions, the placing of a penny on one of them will tip their balance. Replacing and adjusting those on our damaged machine was a major repair task.

Similarly with the tail rotor, a smaller but most important part of the 'copter, which has the task of holding the body of the machine straight against the torque created by the main rotor blades in their counter-clockwise whirling. The pilot controls the tail rotor with foot pedals, increasing its pitch to offset any increase in pitch and increased drag on the main blades. No 'copter can function without the tail rotor. The damage to the hollow tube skid, while extensive, was much less critical.

For signalling rescuers we had the fire, a hand mirror for heliographic use. The three flares would prove a mixed blessing. If they fell short into the bush there was grave danger of fire as the region was tinder-dry, having been without rain for weeks.

We had barely completed our preparations when Brisbin was stirred by the sound of a distant aircraft. Excitedly we discharged the flares, but the plane, a distant speck, gave no sign of recognition.

We were cursing our bad luck when we saw smoke rising from the bush 50 or 60 feet from where we stood. One of the flares had ignited the matted tundra and already the flames were licking around some derelict timber, I grabbed our ration box, scooped up water from a muddy pool in a hollow while Bill tossed dirt on the fire. I looked at how close it was to the 'copter. "I simply have to move the machine to a safer spot," I said.

There wasn't much choice but I settled on a place about 100 feet up the hillside, an open, level, and larger roost for our wounded bird provided it could be made to fly that far.

We offloaded everything and I set about coaxing the 'copter to spread its ruffled wings. Finally it responded, the damaged main blades moving, slowly at first, then with more authority as I manipulated the throttle.

Nursing it along, I persuaded it to lift off the ground a

couple of feet. It settled right back, but not before I had made it move in the direction I wanted. The rotors turned crazily, threatening to tear loose from their housing and offering the grim prospect of beheading anyone who happened to be in the way.

I persisted, sweaty and anxious, and after a few minutes of hop-skip-and-jump I had the 'copter where I wanted it, without further damage. I climbed out, whitefaced and tired, my arms feeling like lead weights from fighting the balky controls. Weary and blackened, we then turned our attention to the fire. We finally got it out.

Confident of rescue but not certain when it might come, we prepared a landing pad for the rescue chopper. We then divided our sandwiches and arranged a schedule so that the signal fire would be attended at all times, for there was a real possibility that some craft might turn up in the darkless night. Several times we heard aircraft engines and stirred the fire into a mighty blaze, without result. It was frustrating, almost nerve-wracking to hear planes flying almost overhead with no indication they could see us. I remember saying to Brisbin—I think I was joking—"the next son of a bitch over will be shot down in flames".

Help, when it arrived, came suddenly about seven o'clock the next morning, in the shape of a Sikorsky S-55 helicopter, a six-passenger machine too large to get down into our narrow stream bed.

"It's Jim Foster," I shouted to Brisbin over the welcome roar of the Sikorsky. Foster waved several times and departed. Now it was just a matter of waiting.

Four or five hours later another Bell helicopter, like ours, put down and Jim Grady stepped out to tell us that the search for us had been going on all night. He had been flying 13 hours without rest, a fact that made him as delighted to see us as we were to shake his hand. Grady, also employed by Okanagan, had responded at once to requests for help, in the search. It was never in question, in fact, for there is a great camaraderie among professional flyers. It was a matter of real regret to lose the friendship of our rescuer some time later in one of those strange mishaps that even the most experienced flyers suffer. Jim, seeking to land close to a

15

rocky outcropping, was instantly killed when one of the main rotor blades struck a rock face, broke, and flew through the cockpit.

The rescue plane had an engineer passenger who quickly assessed the damage to my 'copter. We closely examined the stricken machine while Jim flew Bill back to camp. When Jim returned we all flew out to base camp where we radioed our Vancouver office for spare parts.

The parts were sent on a Canadian Pacific Airlines flight to Whitehorse where Bill Simpson and I picked them up in his Beaver late that night.

On the third day after the crash I joined the two engineers at the wreck site and set to work on the downed Bell. A new $8000 transmission, new main rotor blades and a new tail rotor were installed, as well as a new skid. It was quickly and so expertly done that we might have been in a hangar at a major maintenance base.

One of the things I came to understand as my helicopter flying hours mounted was how fortunate I had been in my first crash. It is seldom that a pilot involved in a major crackup is able to fly out the same machine, fully repaired, within a few days.

As we had waited for our rescuers I told Bill that when we did get back to camp I would spice the occasion with a bottle of vodka that I had carefully hidden away in my kit. I felt it would be one way to say 'sorry' to Bill and those six geologists who had been forced to spend an uncomfortable night in the wilderness wondering about their whirlybird man and what could have happened to him and his machine.

We climbed out at the camp to a raucous reception. Clearly the celebration had begun, apparently with a bottle of Scotch provided by one of my geologist 'victims', Huen Walton. Obviously one bottle wouldn't go far, I thought, so I hurried to my tent to get the vodka. It wasn't there. Back in the mess tent, however, there was a vodka bottle, empty! My engineer had played host. Bill and I settled for coffee which probably was just as well, for I had to get ready for an early takeoff next morning.

The nicest outcome of the whole affair, and a real tribute to my employers, was that no one, then or later, bothered to point out to me that my inexperience had cost the company about $25,000 in repairs and lost time. Far from being critical, I found, company officials gave support and publicly demonstrated this a day or two after my accident.

On returning to camp I spotted our chief flying instructor, Don Poole, down at the landing area. He was so popular a figure that we used to call him 'Dad' and he used to call us some affectionately unprintable names in reply. I thought, Migawd, he's here to give me a blast about the wreck. Putting on the best face I could muster I stepped out of the helicopter and stuck out my hand. "Hi Dad," I said, "How are you?" He grasped my hand firmly, looked me in the eye and replied, "I'm fine, but I couldn't be your dad, I'm married."

The next day we were moving camp and everyone was working. I loaded the chopper with every bit of gear I could, started up, lifted off and made a run down an open space toward a fringe of trees. As they loomed up I realized I wasn't going to get over them. What a spot for a crash, with the chief flying instructor watching. I kicked the controls, turned the chopper as fast as she could move, went back and took another run at it. Once more I found it was doubtful that I could clear. I turned once more, put the machine down and offloaded 70 or 80 pounds. Next time it was easy. I was up and away, all hazard behind me.

I learned later that my performance hadn't worried anyone but my engineer who said, in a loud voice as I finally got away, "Jeesus, what a pilot." Don took the young man by the arm, quietly walked him aside and explained that he disapproved of disparaging remarks of this sort, particularly when they weren't justified, because I had done a hell of a good job in refusing to take chances.

To underline the point, at dinner in the mess hall that night, he waited for a lull in the conversation to remark, in a loud, clear voice, "Charles, you did a great job in handling the machine this morning." I didn't know about his criticism of my engineer at that time but I was appreciative of the sentiment which boosted my morale immensely at a time when it needed a lift. That's what I call leadership, the kind of thing that bosses should do more often, because their associates surely respond to it as I did.

It's a fact that to survive you have to learn quickly as a bush pilot of any kind of machine. That summer gave me a good share of lessons that served all through my flying career.

There was a second unexpected session of instruction not long after my first crash and this time I got out of it with no damage to anyone or anything.

I was assigned to pick up two men from a very small clearing in the bush. They were part of a ground party that had walked in and the area where I had to find them had been burned over by a forest fire that left the trees blackened, fire-hardened spikes so tough you could barely put an axe into them.

It wasn't far to go but I took the usual precautions and filled both my fuel tanks, just in case.

Pilots are taught early to 'top off' their tanks. It not only gives a sense of security but provides a safety margin, an insurance against running out. I am proud to say that in all my years of flying I never experienced this misfortune.

I set down my chopper at the rendezvous and met two men, one young and lanky, the other short and stout, probably in his fifties. They had been taken into the area by ground vehicles and had walked some distance. There was no problem in loading them and within minutes I started up again and quickly cleared the trees. Then I realized there had been a sudden shift in the wind and that I was, in fact, taking off downwind and instead of the chopper rising it was beginning to lose height with alarming rapidity.

It was no time to toss mental coins for a heads-or-tails decision so I headed towards an area where the trees seemed shorter and fewer in number. They were still too close together to make it safe to land and I was obliged to hold the machine hovering just above them, unable to get down or rise.

Quite clearly my problem was weight—two almost full gasoline tanks and three adults. I had several choices, none of them attractive. Providing I could hold the machine as it was for up to 90 minutes I could burn off enough fuel to permit me to lift up and fly away. The prospect of remaining almost motionless for 1½ hours, as the chopper burned off 21 gallons of fuel, each weighing 7.2 pounds, looked remote. Another option was to bleed off enough fuel by opening a tap on the outside of the cabin. I could open this if I could climb out on the skids, but that would leave no one in command of the chopper. I decided that it was inadvisable to ask one of them to climb out and open the fuel tap, for they wouldn't know where it was or how to do it, and might have trouble trying to balance on the carrier, particularly in view of the real chance that vagrant gusts of wind might cause the chopper to buck unexpectedly.

The wind, in fact, was the real danger, for it might throw the machine into contact with one of those ugly black spikes and damage the main rotor or smash the tail rotor, which I could not see because it was directly behind me.

We were about 18 feet in the air all this time, not far from the assured safety of the ground but unable to get down to it. Somehow we had to lighten the plane by more than 100 pounds, and the only way I could conceive it could be accomplished was to get rid of one of the passengers.

I explained our predicament and suggested that it might just be possible for one of the two men to drop from the helicopter to the ground. Immediately the man nearest to the door, the older and heavier of the two, volunteered to try. He weighed a good 170 pounds and if he could be safely offloaded I was sure our troubles were over.

We talked it over very carefully. I explained how he should get out on the skid, moving only inches at a time to give me a chance to correct the helicopter for the shifting of weight, and how he should firmly grasp the skid and slowly lower his body to dangle below it until he could see where he could land without impaling himself on one of those forbidding tree spikes.

He was a game one. He did just as we had planned. When I had lowered the machine as far as I dared, he let go, dropping perhaps a dozen feet to ground. He got up, dusted himself, and waved that he was fine.

That was all we needed. Relieved of the weight the machine went straight up. I flew the other passenger out the eight or 10 miles to camp, then returned to the original clearing where I rendezvoused with the gritty character who bailed out.

His experience didn't seem to have affected him for he climbed aboard without hesitation and was quickly chatting away about the excitement. I congratulated him on his courage and asked him what he thought about the adventure. "It was all right," he replied with a big grin, "although I could say it's a hell of a way for a man to have his first helicopter ride."

The incident embarrassed me, just the same, and I swore my passengers to secrecy. Somehow the story leaked for when I got back to Calgary the company manager called me in. I stood waiting for a blast. Instead he congratulated me, said it was a good show and lauded my solution to a very tricky problem.

# 2

# Sprouting Wings

In retrospect I realize that nature had a lot to do with my becoming an aircraft pilot. The Second World War was more than halfway along when I graduated from high school in my native London, Ontario. That community had long associations with flying, extending back to the grass runways on the Lambeth suburban flying field on which First World War pilots trained.

During the second 'global debate' the air force action was at Crumlin, a military field used as it is today by commercial planes. It lies north of Ontario's Number 2 Highway, one of the historic roads of the region, just east of London, on the Thames River.

Back in the late twenties the district buzzed with flying excitement as two would-be trans-Atlantic flyers readied their single engine plane for a daring non-stop flight to the older London on the other side of a formidable ocean. The Spirit of London was one of a number of planes earmarked for this sort of adventuring and shared the fate of many of them. It lumbered along a four-mile runway cut through farmland south of the highway, struggled into the air and vanished over the Atlantic, never to be heard from again.

Flying was a much more important, better organized business when, one day late in 1942, I reported to the recruiting officer of the Royal Canadian Air Force in London, and told him I would like to be an air gunner.

He looked astonished—with good reason. Gunners were usually of smaller stature than I was. Wireless air gunners—WAGS in the parlance of the day—had a life expectancy even more limited than other bomber crew members as they took the war into Germany from the searchlight studded skies of the Reich. WAGS fought and died, in cramped gun turrets, and their chance of escape from a stricken aircraft, as well as their chance of being shot in the air combat, was unattractive. They were the prime target of the enemy. I volunteered for the job because I wasn't really aware of these grim facts at the time, and because I doubted if I had the qualifications to become a pilot.

The recruiting officer looked at me quizzically. "How tall are you?" "Six foot, two and a half," I replied. "Hell," he laughed, "there's no way you'll ever fit in any gun turret." He thought a minute, then continued, "How would you like to be a pilot?"

It was a minor incident, one that could be matched by any fledgling flyer, but it taught me an excellent lesson: that panic must be fought and overcome and that the flyer who keeps his head has a first rate chance of keeping his health.

At Davidson we had been housed in a two-storey **H** hut in which both male and female R.C.A.F. personnel (completely separated by doorless walls) were quartered.

If boy-met-girl with anything but routine service intentions it had to be off the station. The arrangement, I suspect, led to the first 'streaking' although it hardly went by that name at the time and was involuntary rather than planned.

The washrooms for occupants were in the center connecting arm of the **H** and men going to the showers had to pass by a fire exit door opening to a slide-like chute to the ground.

The temptation was irresistible, especially with the arrival of new squads of recruits, for a posse to lay in wait for the potential bathers as they strolled, clad only in bath towels, to the showers. As they came to the fire door the ambushers would leap upon them with loud shouts, snatch away the towels, and push them through the door down the waiting chute.

At ground level the discomfited would-be bathers, now *au*

*naturel,* would be forced to flee for the nearest entrance to their quarters which happened to be the front door of the male section. These antics were observed by scores of delighted Wids (women's division) recruits who speeded the flight of the victims with shrieks of laughter and observations of a ruder sort.

A refinement of the scheme provided a squad at the front entrance to lock the door just as the naked footracer arrived, forcing him to run clear around the building to the back door. It was sport for the summer, of course. In the winter temperatures fell far below zero.

When I left Davidson I graduated second in my class, and was sent for advanced, or service flying, training to Brandon, Manitoba. There I converted to the twin-engined Cessna Crane, a fabric-covered machine without radio.

Four months at Brandon were routine days of training livened by one exciting occasion when, in forced landing drill, I came within a split second of touching down without having lowered the retractable undercarriage. Fortunately, I was doing a solo at the time and my instructor never became aware of how close his prize pupil had been to a belly-flop.

Failure rates remained constant at all the training schools in my experience. At Brandon, we had some 35 students in my class of which only 22 or 23 graduated. It had little to do with education as some non-university types like me passed. Some graduates from top universities failed.

I think it was mainly a matter of physical co-ordination along with flying determination and keenness, and I was remarkably in earnest.

So there I was, a flyer on the evidence of my instructors, with no place to fly for the moment, a condition shared by a good many more about that time. Some of us were sent on a two-month commando course to Quebec. We weren't needed overseas and it was one way of keeping us busy. I came off that assignment with heightened respect for commandos. It was tough, muscle-building work and I was never fitter in my life than at the end of it.

It might have been almost unbearable because the whole thing was so clearly a make-work affair, but any pain I felt was eased by the fact that I was one of the fortunate half-

23

dozen in my Brandon class to be selected for an officer's commission.

Few things in my life have matched the experience of waking one morning a lowly leading aircraftsman and going to bed that night an officer. One minute you're treated like dirt. You salute everybody and everything. The next minute you're being saluted and ushered into the officers' mess. That's some transition.

I finished my flying training in January, 1944, but didn't fly again until July, when I arrived at an advanced flying school in England and had to learn how to navigate over the vastly different British landscape from a base in Warwickshire.

The war was winding down and it was not my lot to see action. For six months I was a flying instructor and then came D-Day.

Many of us were asked if we wished to volunteer to fly in the war against Japan. To a man we declined the invitation for most had had more than enough of the R.C.A.F. and the ambiguity of being trained to fight but unable to put that training to use. Few believed that the Japanese war could continue long enough to permit them to get into it.

That was an easy question to answer but I warned him that I probably lacked qualifications. He said he would chance that and sent me along through a series of tests that demonstrated that I was, on the contrary, well qualified to become a candidate for pilot training.

A session with the medical officer confirmed my fitness and I was sent off to Toronto for a couple of months of basic training before being shipped away to Mont Joli, Quebec. I travelled to Mont Joli full of excited hopes that soon died under the strain of several months of pointless 'tarmac duty.' Much of this consisted of retrieving drogues shot down by more fortunate recruits in aerial gunnery practice. The drogues fell all over the place, most of the time in deep snow, and could only be picked up after tiring walks on snowshoes; then came the task of counting the bullet holes in them. It seemed a strange route to the romantic assignment of flying an aircraft in combat.

Eventually the system clanked once more and I was sent to

24

Initial Training School (I.T.S.) in Victoriaville, Quebec. This was strictly a ground school teaching navigation, theory of flight, air frame construction and similar basics.

It wasn't until July 19, 1943, that I first put a hand on an airplane. The great moment came at a flying school in Davidson, Saskatchewan. Months of tedium were forgotten when I donned flying gear for my first flight with my instructor in a Cornell tandem two-seater.

Sgt. Pilot Long, an American, took one look at the gangling Canadian youngster and noted his surface air of confidence. "Have you ever flown before?" he asked. I suspect his motives now, but I didn't at the time. And I didn't want to appear too green. "I've had about 10 hours in commercial craft," I replied. "Fine," said Long, "then perhaps you'd like to do some aerobatics?" I swallowed hard and agreed that I would.

Several thousand feet up he told me on the intercom to tighten my safety belt. I hadn't the faintest idea how that was done! In my fumbling I unlocked the harness, just as Long began a series of loops and rolls. All I could do was hang on grimly to the safety harness and pray that my small fib would be overlooked by the great judge of flying recruits.

My stay at Davidson was relatively unexciting except for one flight towards the end of my course. I had flown solo in about eight hours, a normal time in the training schedule of the R.C.A.F., and I soon gained confidence. I frequently was up on my own, as I was on this occasion. My training had led me to aerobatics and I was enjoying myself with them within sight of the airfield when I noticed some heavy, low clouds drifting into the area. We had no radios but pilots were recalled by activation of the rotating beacon on top of the control tower. Within a few minutes it was flashing but I decided there was time for two or three more loops. When I finally levelled out I found I was very wrong. The airfield had vanished in low cloud.

Loss of contact with the ground can be a source of genuine panic and for a moment I experienced it as I tried to pierce the overcast and found I could see nothing in any direction. I recalled that the railway line ran beside the town and the airfield and all I had to do was get above the cloud and look

25

for a break in it to get down in the clear and locate the steel lines. I soon rose above the cloud blanket and after some minutes I found a hole large enough to permit me to descend. I had no worries about heights for the area was almost flat with no hills or mountains to worry about.

Sure enough, the comfort-giving railway right-of-way was quickly spotted. I began to follow it with a confidence that slowly waned as I realized that I did not recognize any of the landmarks that were appearing. Once more I reasoned it out, deciding that I had been flying in the wrong direction, something easy enough to do in sunless conditions such as those prevailing under the cloud cover. A glance at the fuel tank indicator reassured me so I banked and reversed my course. My faith in those railway tracks held firm.

Eventually the familiar outline of Davidson appeared and I turned north and followed the road that led to the air station. I was only a few hundred feet up and there wasn't another plane in the air. Also, I was more than an hour overdue and I found a worried group in the crew room trying to determine in what wheat field I must have crashed.

Certainly life as a civilian was more attractive than peacetime military service so I mustered out with a minimum of regret.

For some years I was satisfied to work for a soft drink company in southwestern Ontario, a satisfaction that slowly and continuously declined. In 1951, thirsting for something more adventurous, I returned to the R.C.A.F. My posting was one of instructor for younger men whom I taught to fly in Harvards, Expediters and Mitchell B-25s. It was a tremendous thrill to be airborne once more and I experienced, at first, an infinite sense of liberation and exhilaration: that soaring of the soul that every flyer has known up in the wild blue where not even the eagles climb.

Unfortunately, I found there was a vast difference between the R.C.A.F. in war and in peace. The peace-time air force, to be brutally frank about it, is the married man's dish with routine rules, and where enthusiasm is not encouraged. Everything had to be done through channels. Promotion was by seniority, and frequently by judicious back-slapping and boot-licking—not according to ability.

The presence of families sprinkled the whole military machine with an air of domesticity that was unreal in what should have been a force, fit and ready to fight.

I was unmarried, and had no domestic constraints. Adventure still beckoned with no place to go in uniform after the brief scramble of the Korean war. In 1956, with some regret because I was acknowledging the truth of a vanished hope, I surrendered my commission, slightly ahead of the expiry term of five years for which I had enlisted.

Looking back I find it a time that distressed me, not only for my lost dream but from my concern about the low estate into which the R.C.A.F. had fallen in comparison with the proud force it had been little more than a decade earlier. One experience will illustrate what I mean. I was flying out of Saskatoon, instructing eager young men in the flying of Mitchell bombers. They attracted my interest, for in them I saw myself a few years earlier. They had not been infected with the dry rot of peacetime service as I had been; they were willing and most anxious to succeed. I was airborne just after takeoff with a student when power failed in the left engine. I saw that the oil seal on the propeller constant speed unit had blown out, and within seconds the engine was on fire.

Although my student was showing commendable coolness, I took over the plane and headed back for a landing, reporting the condition of my plane in a radio call to the control tower, which they acknowledged. I told them of my plan for an emergency landing.

"Do you want a crash truck?" the controller asked.

I suggested it would be a wise precaution and that they might provide an ambulance, too, just in case, because the plane was now trailing a dense cloud of smoke even though the engine fire extinguisher had been released, and with only one engine, operating at nearly full power, the landing might be a difficult one.

Down we came, smoke pouring from the damaged engine. We landed successfully, turned off the runway and quickly jumped from the plane and looked around.

We were quite alone. There was no reception committee, no sign of a crash truck, no ambulance. Somehow, they had never been alerted.

27

Fortunately, they weren't needed, but that was hardly to the credit of the control tower. The contrast between the alertness of the wartime R.C.A.F. and the slackness of the peacetime service was on display for the few who cared to see.

What angered me more than anything was the realization that some people didn't care. As I came into the hangar I noticed several officers talking. They seemed light-hearted enough in contrast to the way I felt.

I noticed that the group included the station commander, the chief flying instructor, the chief of maintenance, and an air vice-marshal who was visiting the station. As I approached I heard the chief flying instructor assuring the AVM that this was the first time the crash trucks hadn't arrived promptly in response to a call at that landing strip.

Everyone there outranked me, a lowly flying officer, but my hackles were up. "That's bullshit, sir," I said, "I've been here three years and never once in that time have I known the crash trucks to be there on time."

I'm sure the AVM believed me, by the look on his face as he regarded the red countenances around him.

Three weeks later I was summarily posted to Centralia in Western Ontario, removed from instructing recruits in flying B-25s to return to instruction on Harvard trainers. There may be some reward in Heaven for telling the truth. Frequently, on this side of the Great Divide, it is clear there is not.

After my final doffing of the uniform I worked for a Vancouver insurance company. I was often close enough to the expanding Vancouver International airport to be stirred by the growing activity there.

Even more intriguing to me than the new, monster, civilian planes were the increasing number of helicopters on the tarmac. One day in 1957, while visiting the flying club, I struck up a conversation with the chief flying instructor about the impressive row of Okanagan Helicopter machines visible from the lounge.

"I'd sure like to have a whirl with one of those some day," I said. He looked at me and saw I was in earnest. "Have you met anyone with Okanagan?" he asked. I told him that I had not. "Well, come along then," he added, and in a few seconds I was shaking hands with Carl Agar, boss of what was at that time the largest commercial helicopter company in the world.

Okanagan had been started on the thinnest of shoestrings back in 1946 when Agar and his partner Alf Stringer were slowly starving to death operating a small flying school. They begged, borrowed and scratched up $45,000 to buy their first 'copter—and never looked back. By the time I was talking to Agar the firm had more than 50 machines in service, and had established an international reputation. Stringer hasn't done badly for himself either. He now operates and owns Vancouver Island Helicopters, with 10 machines flying regularly out of Patricia Bay at the Victoria International Airport.

Agar introduced me to Fred Snell, his chief pilot. I told them of my interest in becoming a helicopter pilot. They were courteous and details of my flying experience interested them. They told me they were looking for former fixed-wing pilots with lots of flying time, and my service record appeared to suit them. I made the customary application for employment, expecting to be called in a short time. Weeks passed and I began checking every day to see where I stood. Finally, perhaps in desperation to end my inquiries, I was told that I could become a student in their Kamloops, B.C., training school.

My first helicopter flight, in a Bell 47-G1 with Okanagan's chief instructor Don Poole, was a memorable experience. We flew down the lovely Fraser Valley, its mountain borders assuming a new meaning to me in this unusual craft. It seemed unreal at first, like sitting in a revved-up flying carpet, and I fell in love with whirlybirds at first flight.

In that three-month course starting in Kamloops and concluding in Penticton I learned to fly a helicopter as well as you can without actually getting out into the wilds and doing all the things we were taught. When the course ended I had logged more than 75 flying hours and learned some important things exclusively the requirements of 'copter flying. Things like landing in restricted areas, on little hummocks and on mountain ledges where an error would mean a drop off into hundreds, even thousands, of feet of nothing but air. We were meticulously drilled and our class soon found that it was a much more exacting science than flying fixed-wing craft, one calling for additional and unexpected skills.

Part of the drill was learning to put the machine down in very small open spaces, with as little as eight or 10 feet clearance for the rotors. It was fun, in a way, for we would be cruising along when Don Poole would spot a likely area and have me put down at once. We came down in some strange places. One day Don insisted that I ground the machine in a backyard behind an apparently abandoned farmhouse in the Fraser Valley.

It was a tight squeeze but I made it. We were sitting there for a minute with the rotors idling when suddenly the back door of the house opened and a woman looked out. She eyed us up, down and sideways and her face was expressionless. After a minute or two she went back into the house and closed the door, as if helicopter visitations were an everyday event. We were obviously more astonished by her reaction than she had been by our sudden appearance.

There is some similarity between 'copters and conventionals, of course. When you push the controls forward you dive and when you pull them backward you climb. But the physical side of directing a 'copter is completely different.

In a helicopter you have to learn to do five things at once with only four control appendages. You use both feet, one on each rudder pedal to control the tail rotor pitch. Your right hand grasps a stick that comes up from the floor between your legs. It is called the cyclic and, when manipulated, it alters the path of the main rotor blades and tilts the whole rotor system according to the direction in which it is moved.

Think of the rotors not as two separate blades, but as one plate which can be tilted upwards, sideways, backwards or down. If you are flying level and pull it back you climb. If you push it forward you descend. Hold it back long enough and you come to a stop and start to back up, something that requires more power than moving ahead.

With your left hand you control a stick called a collective,

**30**

which comes up from the left side of the pilot's seat. Pull up on this and the pitch increases on the main rotor blades, making the machine ascend at a speed dependent on the amount of extra pitch and power applied.

Also with the left hand, you manipulate a throttle grip similar to that on the handlebars of a motorcycle, a twist control that increases or decreases your engine power.

In a Bell like those I used much of the time, you prepare for liftoff by increasing your power until you are at 3200 engine revolutions per minute, which produces about 200 r.p.m. of the main rotor blades. As you pull up you increase the pitch on the main rotor blades which increases the drag so you have to twist the left hand control to increase power to maintain the correct rotor revolutions.

This, in turn, increases the torque, so you apply left rudder to increase the compensating pitch on the tail rotor. If you didn't, the body of the machine would go in a direction opposite to the main rotor system.

And while you're doing five things with four manipulating extensions you also have to keep an eye on the instruments to make sure you stay within 200 r.p.m. of the number needed, for you must not go below 3000 engine r.p.m., otherwise the main rotor blades will flex because there is insufficient centrifugal force to keep them straight.

The vital point is the red line on the manifold pressure gauge. This warns of power demands beyond safe limits.

As you can now imagine, this is a most demanding exercise for a new pilot who finds, too, that when he is airborne he must be much more delicate with the controls than is the case in a fixed-wing. It's more a pressure than a direct push or pull and to the passengers so little of the control requirement is visible they get the idea that flying a 'copter is a piece of cake.

Actually there is no way you can convert from fixed-wing to rotating wings in the three or four hours that it takes to make the move from one conventional craft to another. In fixed-wings after four hours or so flying, you're safe, and while you may not be an ace you can fly the new plane. There are just too many variables in the switch to a helicopter. It takes a good many hours of flying experience before you can jump into one of them and go just as you do in your car.

Takeoff and landing are the most difficult functions, although you learn in landing to appreciate the value of the air cushion effect that is created by the rotors compressing the air by pushing the air down as you approach the ground. In fact, in this denser air you actually land in a cushion and can come straight down fully loaded.

Lifting off is something else. You go up a foot or two and then you start to move forward to a point where at 20 to 21 miles an hour you go through what is called translational lift. This is where the air flow through the main rotor blades creates increased lift. The eventual departure is sudden, a swoop into the air. It can be straight up when the chopper is lightly loaded, without the necessity of travelling forward.

Air temperatures have to be considered. Hot air is thinner and more difficult to work in. If it's really cold—say 40° below zero—the air is denser and you don't need as much takeoff space. But nothing in the book quite explains how these factors work. You must get to know them from experience.

In restricted liftoff areas you have to be alert to kick left rudder and make a fast about-turn if there is any doubt about clearing the area. You usually apply left rudder not because right rudder wouldn't work but because you're seated on the left side of the chopper and can see where you're turning as that side dips. Often you can get off just by making a quick about turn and going the other way. If you can't you do another turn, face the wind and sit down, trying again after offloading some cargo.

This doesn't occur much in mountain flying. When you land on a ridge there are seldom any trees to contend with but you must remember the thin air at height, unless you have a super-charged or jet engine.

In the early days we used to land quite close to the edge of a mountain and fall off so that it was simply a case of over-revving about 200 r.p.m.—enough to lift you off the ground—and literally falling over the side. In fact, you jumped off into space. Once your forward speed got with you, a matter of seconds, you were away. It was scary for new passengers because they didn't really know what was going on. And looking back at it from a distance of 15 years, I can only say I wouldn't want to be doing it now.

But the helicopter world is changing. Jet engines have revolutionized the business. There are, and for some time will be, a lot of normally aspirated and super-charged conventional engines around simply because they are too valuable to be discarded and operators can't afford to sell them off to buy expensive jets. The day is not far away, however, when almost all choppers will be jet-propelled and the conventionals that I flew will be as rare as a model T Ford.

When I first began flying helicopters we had no crash locator devices, primarily because they cost about $1000 each and a fleet installation was beyond the resources of most firms.

A crash locator is a radio device that is activated by a severe shock such as a crash landing. It immediately begins sending a signal on a distress frequency and can be picked up by search aircraft who home in on it and locate the crash site, even if the crew and passengers are disabled. Under favorable conditions it has a range up to 60 miles and undoubtedly many lives have been saved, and much expense avoided, by this most useful invention.

Today, although choppers are much more expensive, the cost of a locator is about $200 and no aircraft should be permitted to fly unless one is installed and working. Hundreds of thousands of dollars are spent many times a year in air searches for lost planes and people. In Canada, I claim, the government could afford to equip every aircraft with a crash locator and wind up money ahead in the Search and Rescue business.

I've been caught up in a number of these searches and the expense is just fantastic. Anyone who can afford to fly an airplane can afford $200 and shouldn't be permitted to take off without placing that cheap and vital insurance policy not only on the lives of himself and his passengers but on the lives of the many who may be imperilled through hunting for him. Many pilots and crews have been killed searching for downed aircraft. Today all new aircraft must be equipped with crash locator beacons.

33

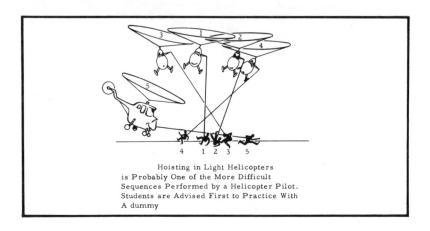

Hoisting in Light Helicopters
is Probably One of the More Difficult
Sequences Performed by a Helicopter Pilot.
Students are Advised First to Practice With
A dummy

# 3

# The Seal Hunt

Millions of people have experienced a feeling of deep revulsion as they have watched on television, and read about, the annual slaughter of thousands of harp seal pups on the ice off the east coast of Canada.

I share their instinctive horror at the practice, although I do not subscribe to the conclusion of the most vocal critics who demand that the hunt be banned by international agreement. I approach the controversy from a much closer viewpoint than most. For two seasons I flew a seal hunt helicopter and got to know the men who conduct the hunt, and the methods they use.

Few experiences in my flying career have been as fascinating as this annual seal hunt—a bloody, smelly, chilly, lucrative business founded on one of the basic human instincts, now perversely adapted to the provision of vanity furs for the luxury trade of an affluent world. Once it was a necessity for the preservation and nourishment, the food and clothing, of Canadian maritimers, but only indirectly today does the seal hunt feed and clothe those who participate in it.

I had changed jobs and early in 1963 was employed by Spartan Helicopters, an Ottawa-based firm with western headquarters in Calgary. I was asked if I would take an assignment flying with the sealing fleet out of Newfoundland. Spartan, a company flying some 20 choppers, had provided helicopters for the hunt in previous years and was looking for experienced pilots for what officials admitted was a tiring and hazardous flying job.

The season lasted only four weeks, usually beginning on March 10 each year, and the short duration of the hunt meant that there were few who had any experience in this kind of flying. It required the ability to land a helicopter on a small platform on the stern of the sealers, and to navigate by compass and celestial observation over wide expanses of ice with no real landmarks but the ships. Any pilot with the sealing fleet needed all these qualities and a vital plus, an ability not to panic in tight situations.

I agreed to take the assignment and went to company headquarters in Ottawa for my briefing and to pick up my chopper. For reasons that still puzzle me, (I doubt if they have ever done it since and probably never had before) they decided against flying the aircraft to Newfoundland and arranged to move it on a 40-foot trailer towed by a half-ton truck.

My own preference was to fly the craft East in easy stages but I accepted the decision and started out in late February on what turned out to be a nightmare journey. The highway was covered with ice and snow. In the Maritimes we ran into late winter storms that delayed, and finally halted us. Worst of all, I found I had been saddled with an engineer with a fatal weakness, an inability to pass up a drink or the opportunity to buy one.

A tow and some hard digging freed us and we drove to Sydney, N.S., where we boarded the ferry for the extremely rough crossing of the Cabot Straits.

We were due to rendezvous with our lessee, a tough Newfoundlander named Guy Earle, (I like to think of him as the last of the glamorous buccaneers) and sail with him on his sealer, the Kyle, from Carbonear, on the east coast of Newfoundland on March 9. We drove up to the only hotel in Port aux Basques in the midst of a howling snowstorm. It promised to be a cold night, for the hotel furnace had gone on strike. Fortunately, my engineer and I managed to make a quick repair job for the distressed hosteler, who demon-

36

strated his gratitude by sending a gift bottle of whisky to my room.

Next morning, with the weather moderating, we ventured out to the helicopter where the engineer installed the main rotor and tail blades, which had been removed for the long road journey. The improvement in conditions tempted me to make a test flight and I lifted the machine into the air from the trailer and after about a 15-minute test flight landed on the parking lot of the hotel.

My engineer had disappeared and it was some minutes before I thought to check his room. There I found him reclining on his bed, a full glass of our gift whisky in his hand, and clear indication that a sizable portion of it had preceded that monumental 'shot'. I snatched the glass from his hand, poured it down the sink and returned to my room where I telephoned head office in Ottawa and informed Spartan I would proceed no farther with this obviously untrustworthy associate.

They told me to stay where I was and I waited a full day until Spartan's chief engineer flew out from Ottawa. He heard my story, inspected the helicopter and to his dismay found a number of improperly-placed bolts that could have sheared off or fallen off in flight, as well as improperly adjusted rotors and improper cable tensions.

There was no questions that I would have to be provided with a new engineer. My actions may have seemed imperious but where the life of the passengers and the pilot are at stake there can be no temporizing with the inadequate.

Spartan, to give the company full marks, immediately flew out an engineer from Calgary as a replacement, and he caught up with me at Corner Brook two days later—just enough delay to make us miss our rendezvous with the **Kyle**.

At Carbonear, Capt. Earle had left a detaiied message arranging a rendezvous at sea, somewhere in the seal-bearing ice floes off the coast of Labrador. It was a bit like looking for the proverbial haystack needle but I had one thing to guide me that few other ships could have offered. The **Kyle** was a former Canadian Pacific Railway coastal ship, about 250 feet long and some 1500 tons. Her profile was not unlike dozens of sealers in the fleet but almost alone among them she was a coal burner, and the black message pouring from her stack would write my directions to her flight deck as accurately as anything that might have been devised for visual recognition.

Not being certain where the energetic Earle had gone, I had to consider the problem of refueling. Assured that I would find fuel at Mary's Harbor, on the Labrador coast, I charted a flight plan for a stop there.

It should have been easy to find, I suppose, but the truth is I couldn't locate that very small pinpoint of a settlement in the vast white expanse of the land God gave to Cain, and to this day I have never set eyes on it.

I had been told that there were storage tanks around the port—a sort of "you-can't-miss-it" identification. The truth is that you can miss it, as anyone who has been tendered that sort of encouragement knows very well. I flew up every inlet on the coast as they appeared, and fuel was getting dangerously low when I spotted a cluster of houses in a small bay, with two gray tanks on a nearby hill.

"That's it," I thought, "although the tanks aren't that close to the waterfront." I was wrong. It was an even smaller hamlet than Mary's Harbor, about 15 miles south of my elusive destination. And I didn't have enough fuel to complete the trip.

The helicopter's landing brought every able-bodied person in the place down to greet the visitors. They told me there were two 45-gallon drums of 115/145 octane aviation fuel left on a deserted helicopter pad on the hill, the relics of a former U.S. radar base used during the Second World War. I reasoned that if any fuel was left its quality would have declined to a less tigerish octane rating that my machine could use! I flew to the nearby hilltop and landed on the old pad. I tapped the drums, filled up and started the motor. The machine performed perfectly and, having topped off my tanks, I flew out to sea looking for the **Kyle** and its smoke signals.

Sure enough, it was out there, and in little more than an hour I set down my chopper on the small helicopter pad that had been hastily built on the stern of the vessel.

Capt. Earle was delighted and relieved to greet me for the

prospect of conducting the hunt without a helicopter was a dim one in the highly competitive nature of the venture. With the help of his chopper the **Kyle** took aboard 18,000 pelts in that four-week season. Not a bad haul for a small ship, considering that pelts were worth about $50 each.

That harvest of more than $900,000 was one to cheer the 106 sealers on the **Kyle** whose financial return was based on a share of the total proceeds.

That was the good luck of the sealing draw. The second season, 1963, was much different. It was a month of many problems starting with a delay of the official opening of the hunt, arranged by the mutual agreement of the hunters. The seals had arrived late. The pups were small, too young to be of much use in the fur market. A wireless conference among the captains resulted in an agreement for a four-day delay in the opening of the hunt.

It seems little enough but baby seals grow at a prodigious rate nourished entirely on the rich milk of the mother seals. One reason why the hunt is so short, aside from the desirability of controlling the 'farming' of this resource, is the fact that within that time the pups grow immensely and their prized, all-white fur becomes mottled as their size increases, and loses much of its commercial value.

The second year was not a total disaster for the sealers as we finally took in some 8000 pelts, but cut the hunt short several days because of a scarcity of seals and ice conditions that were seldom better than difficult and often much worse.

There were upwards of 70 ships in the sealing fleets in those years, mostly Norwegian, Canadian and Russian. The Soviets preferred to keep well apart from the rest and operated from a large factory ship into which the entire seal was taken and processed, with nary a scrap of the animal wasted.

In the case of the rest of us only the pelts were taken, the rest of the carcass being left to rot on the ice, a shameful waste.

In good years sealers would find as many as 4000 to 5000 seals on a half-mile square of ice. Helicopters had revolutionized the hunting, making the location of the herds much quicker and easier and the transportation of the hunters to the seal floes a simple matter of minutes where it might have taken hours or even days.

Addition of helicopters (by that time no ship was without one) had added an efficiency that was devastating and that has brought about a ban on their use. The simple truth is that the seals were in danger of extermination within a few years because of the ease with which they could be taken and the numbers that were slaughtered.

Without helicopters, ships had to buck the ice until they located the seals visually from the vessel, after which they had to crunch their way through the floes until they could set the hunters down close enough for them to walk to their quarry. One hunter could only haul back two or three pelts at a time, and the hours spent in coming and going were a large part of the relatively brief period of daylight available for the hunt.

The helicopter pilot was the eyes of the hunting ship, scanning the ice for miles around for the telltale dots of the mother seals. They located the herds, radioed the information back to the ship, which immediately headed for the area, and the hunters were dressed ready to be transported to the scene of the discovery within minutes of the receipt of the information.

During the night my helicopter rested precariously on the tiny pad Earle had had built on the stern of the **Kyle,** a windy perch so constricted that I had to leave the tail protruding beyond the stern because of two stern mast guy wires that blocked off the safer area to which it might have been turned. Even at that they offered a hazard for they allowed only about 12 inches of clearance for my 35-foot main rotors, a safety factor so small I persuaded Earle to remove the wires, which he did with some reluctance. To my relief the mast remained upright for I had visions of it falling over the main deck. But it was difficult to service the chopper and when that was necessary we had to lift off and drop onto a flat sheet of ice somewhere close by when the ship was halted.

Once aloft, with the hunters placed, my work went on until dusk for it was my duty to retrieve the pelts and fly them back to the ship where they were dropped on the ice beside the **Kyle.** It was grinding work. I have brought in

40

more than 2000 pelts in a single day, flying a record, for me, of 350 sorties in more than 10 hours of steady flying, halted only by a few minutes here and there to refuel. There was no lunch break. I ate cold sandwiches in the air, or in brief moments on the ice.

Keeping helicopters in flying trim under these circumstances is a triumph of engineering skill and of fortitude. My engineer was up 90 minutes earlier than anyone else every morning—which meant that he was out of the sack at 4:30 a.m. He went directly to the flight deck at the aft end of the ship and set up a tarpaulin shield, a windbreaker covering the helicopter cabin. Behind that, his fingers numb with cold, he had to start a Herman-Nelson, a large gasoline heater from which hot air is forced by a fan. It sounded like a giant blowtorch but it warmed things up enough to make the chopper serviceable by the time it was needed. By that time the engineer was shivering with cold and would come back with his hands and face nipped by frost.

Repairs, which took longer, had to be carried out in the same circumstances. When you read about helicopters aiding the seal hunt you ought to understand that the engineers are the unsung heroes of the performance.

Meals were pretty much of a grab-and-run matter when the sealing was good. On the **Kyle** breakfast usually consisted of salt pork, hardly my idea of high cuisine.

In fact, I refused to eat it and used to ask for, and get, poached eggs which I ate with relish until the morning I took a seat with a view down the passageway to the galley. The cook, a somewhat unkempt, unwashed performer, had cooked my eggs and was bringing them to me on a plate. Part way along he stopped by some slop pails, took the lid off one of them, tipped up the plate and drained off some water, holding the eggs in place with a dirty-looking hand.

I didn't say anything but for the rest of the voyage I ordered my eggs soft-boiled which ensured that they were untouched by human hands until I opened them. Fortunately for me this manner of serving was much less annoying to the galley dictator than my insistence on poached eggs.

On the seal hunt the supreme arbiter is weather, and some days my log book showed as little as a single hour aloft.

While the seals were in their prime the merciless pursuit of the babies went on across several hundred square miles of ice, some of it up to 19 feet thick in places. This may sound like a solid platform on which to work. I thought so, briefly, until I realized that this monstrous mass moves with the tide, groaning and cracking and making odd, primeval noises, as if in agony and revulsion at the things that were being done to its inoffensive marine inhabitants.

Much of the hunt went on inside or near the 12-mile limit within which Canada claimed total sovereignty, although the presence of our national authority was almost invisible. It could be seen fleetingly in the occasional patrol plane in the sky but was seldom demonstrated by the presence of official ships on the sealing grounds. Officialdom, for the most part, was represented in the several ice-breaking ships in federal service, the **Sir John A. Macdonald,** the **Sir Humphrey Gilbert,** and there was no naval representation on regular call.

The Canadians resented the incursions of foreign ships inside the 12-mile limit but there was little they could do about it. Occasionally a trespassing vessel would be spotted, at which point Earle would get on the ship's radio and start talking to his home base in coded messages that alerted headquarters in Carbonear to the presence of intruders, without alarming the miscreants themselves. This device was a necessity, for all the ships kept a constant wireless watch and there were no transmissions that were secret unless in code.

Eventually word got to the federal authorities but by the time they ordered up an aerial inspection craft the offender usually had vanished. Air patrols could intervene, warning off the trespassers by radio as they flew over them, but not many were disciplined although they could be arrested and fined if the offence was flagrant, and a few were handled in this way.

Life aboard a sealer is grim, almost primitive, for the hunt is the whole of its existence. Many of the hunters worked and slept without taking off their clothes. They returned exhausted from their day on the ice, summoned up the energy to satisfy the demands of empty bellies, then collapsed on their bunks. Drinking was strictly forbidden, for obvious reasons, and the men were satisfied to let carousing await the day of their return home.

All the ships had the same life pattern. The **Kyle** was no better off, and no worse, than the others. The sealers devoted their entire existence for the full month to the hunt, in the interests of themselves and their families, for their economic condition for a 12-month period depended largely on the success or failure of their efforts in the few days available to them on the ice.

Sealers, and, to an even greater degree, the captains of sealing ships, have to be dauntless and resourceful. Guy Earle was both, blessed as well with an extra share of native cunning.

He demonstrated that during my second hunt with him when we had been stuck in ice for six days, with production down to a minimum. Seals were scarce and the weather was mostly atrocious. The floes were so heavy the ship was unable to move in the direction of the hunt and the reported location of the seals. Delay was costing $1000 a day, plus the loss of a potential harvest of furs.

After nearly a week of icebound deadlock I flew off some hunters. They were several miles distant with the **Kyle** still unable to do more than thresh about angrily in the same small piece of water. As the day wore on conditions worsened and there was a prospect that I might not be able to retrieve the hunting parties. Earle seized his opportunity, cannily calling on the radio for the assistance of the **Sir John A. Macdonald,** the pride of the ice-breaking fleet and the future savior of the U.S. mammoth oil tanker, the **Manhattan,** in its Arctic adventures a few years later.

Earle besought the Sir John A. to free him from the ice so that he could move toward his endangered hunters. It was getting dark, he pleaded, and they were in danger of being forced to stay all night on the ice in freezing temperatures. The Macdonald responded, crashing along to the **Kyle** with the impact of its reinforced plating and the power of the 19,000 HP engines it could call upon.

The big ship cracked the ice like Thor's hammer, setting the **Kyle** free at last. Earle courteously thanked the Macdonald's captain, who was not the least bit deceived. He knew that he had been duped and proceeded to dress down Earle in the best seagoing fashion. The Macdonald had responded because it could not gamble that Earle was totally deceitful, and he was not. The big ship was delegated to answer a call where danger to the sealers was involved despite the strong possibility that it would have desirable financial consequences, with which the government vessel had no concern, for the **Kyle** and its crew.

In the conditions of the hunt at the time helicopters were an incalculable asset and maintenance was a necessity that simply could not be neglected.

We tried to carry as many spare parts as possible in order to effect repairs without delay but it was impossible to foresee all the needs and it would have been physically impossible to move a complete inventory. Once in a while, then, it was necessary to order spare parts from Ottawa by radio, for air delivery, an advanced art not mastered by many of those attempting it.

As a rule, the parts arrived in a bundle, well padded, to be dropped from the air to the waiting engineer. Because they came in conventional planes there was no opportunity for the delivery craft to land. The secret was to make a 'soft' drop, and few had learned how. We had our helicopter on an ice pan near the **Kyle** one day when the delivery plane appeared. The proper method was a low drop at the slowest possible speed. This pilot stayed well up, and tossed out the bundle while his machine was doing about 150 miles an hour.

We saw it tumbling down, and scattered for safety. The container, as we knew it would, burst like a water bomb, scattering 'shrapnel' in all directions, and strewing parts, nuts, bolts and other hardware over a quarter-mile of hummocks. The comments of the search party sent out to find them were loud and, even in this permissive era, mostly unprintable.

In two seasons of service with him my admiration for Guy Earle continued to grow. He was a born leader, with the quaint speech and habits of the Newfoundlander but a mind as sharp as an ice pick and the business instincts of a Wall Street trader. This shrewdness was matched, as well, by prowess in a number of frontier qualities. He was, for example, a superb shot with a rifle, something he demonstrated to my complete satisfaction one day in the Straits of Belle Isle.

In the course of flying out to the hunting grounds among very hummocky floes only a mile or two from the Labrador shore I saw four large dogs on the ice, savaging small seals. I hovered to look at them and saw their mouths were dripping blood. They were a fearsome sight, absolutely unafraid of the intruder in the sky. As I moved off I saw them turn and stalk in the direction of the seal hunters, who were totally unaware of them. The hunters operated in teams of two and if set upon suddenly by four wild dogs any pair of them might be severely injured or even killed.

I notified Earle by radio of the danger and he ordered me to return at once to the **Kyle** where I found him waiting to join me, armed with a rifle, his pockets bulging with cartridges.

He agreed that the dogs presented a genuine danger and said he would make sure it was eliminated. I set him down behind some ice hummocks in the line of approach the dogs were taking. He lay belly flat on the ice, sighting on the dogs from an icy arm rest. One by one he picked them off—four shots, and four dead dogs. They were half-wild animals that had wandered into the banquet table of the seal hunt from a nearby native village, hell bent for trouble until this modern Robin Hood had dispatched them with an absolute minimum of ammunition.

Earle was some man. I think he liked me in return, for my admiration was obvious. It was a rapport that enabled our association to stand firm under a couple of tricks I played on him.

The first Sunday I spent under his command was a bright, sunny day, perfect for the hunt, and Earle was anxious to get things under way at the earliest possible moment. I turned up for breakfast casually clad, and saw his eyebrows lift. I sat down and started what appeared to be a leisurely breakfast. Earle shifted uneasily, itching to get started, and made strange throat-clearing noises. Finally he got around to making his point—he thought I was taking too long to get under way.

"Oh, didn't you know?" I replied. "I never fly on Sunday. I never do any work on Sunday. It's against my religion."

Earle was bowled over by the thought, almost speechless as he pondered the enormity of the announcement that could remove four working days from 30 and cost him thousands of dollars in pelts as well as several thousand more in fees for an idled helicopter.

His face worked and he looked ready to explode but I kept a straight face and insisted that it was a fact. Earle spluttered, waving his arms. It was impossible to continue. I broke into laughter and assured him I was joking. He was relieved enough, and good enough sport, to join in the belly laughs around the ward room that had accompanied his victimization. I think I liked him from that minute on. He had proved he was more than a good captain, that he was in fact an extra special sort of human being.

# 4

# Killing Ground

That first seal hunt was to have been my last for I returned from Newfoundland determined to abandon the gypsy way of the professional pilot, confident I had found my true vocation and life-work managing an electronics business in the bustling Peace River community of Grande Prairie.

Settling down looked most attractive at that time, particularly in view of what had happened to me and my new bride, Ingeborg, after our marriage in Calgary on June 30, 1962. We had been going out for some time but I found my job with Autair on the Mid-Canada Line left me little time to be with Ingeborg. On June 18 I flew to Calgary from Winisk, determined to quit helicopter flying and get into something that would provide real domesticity and an opportunity to live an orderly life like most other married folk.

I was enjoying my first week as a newlywed when, on July 6, Spartan Helicopters, with whom I worked previously, rang in with a heavy plea for my services to work on a major fire emergency job at La Tuque, Que., where a forest fire was out of control. They assured me the job would last only a few days, and their pleading was so effective that Ingeborg sent me off to the disaster scene with her blessing.

I hurried to Ottawa, picked up a helicopter and rushed to LaTuque. It was all the fire they had promised, raging over 80 square miles, and I worked overtime flying men and equipment to the areas of most immediate danger. Hundreds of ground workers battled the blaze. Water bombers worked long hours dousing the most critical areas. The fire was treacherous. It would leap acres at a time, making it hard to fight or plan to control.

One of the most hair-raising events befell the driver and children in a school bus proceeding down a dirt road that was believed to be safe to use.

Without warning the driver found his way ahead blocked by flames. He turned the bus on the narrow road and headed back. Half-a-mile down the road the fire suddenly jumped the barrier and blocked his retreat. The bus was trapped.

Fortunately, a plane spotted its predicament and radioed to the command post. Water bombers were diverted to the spot and concentrated on putting out the fire at one end so the bus could escape. It got out after some heroics by the bombers. Otherwise the helicopters would have had to risk setting down on that road and picking up the bus passengers. It could have been done but in the strange draft patterns of a major fire it would not have been easy.

Tired, and still smelling of smoke, I got back to Calgary on July 18 hoping to resume that interrupted honeymoon. A day later I was off again on another promised 'short-term' emergency job with a seismic party around Scatter Lake, Hay River and Buffalo Lake. One emergency followed another, relentlessly, in Peace River and elsewhere. Ingeborg, back at work at CFAC, Calgary, stole away for a 'five-day' weekend at Peace River to celebrate my birthday on August 4.

After that it was total separation and hard slogging for both of us. Ingeborg was required to work nights to make up for her unauthorized holiday, and my tour in the bush country went on and on until mid-October.

It wasn't what had been promised me, and my temper grew shorter with the declining hours of daylight. On September 24 I flew out to High Prairie to make a telephone complaint to the company office in Calgary.

That must have been one of the most expensive calls Spartan ever paid for. It was three hours by air each way plus the charge for the call. I figured out that it cost the company

$648 to have me tell them how unhappy I was.

Finally, on October 11, we got a signal to begin moving out the equipment. It was none too soon. There was frost every night and snowfalls that made the tent walls sag. We had been working on the far side of Loon Lake from the access road and that meant most of the heavy gear had to be lifted in and out by chopper, including a box five feet square in which the sensitive seismic blast measuring instruments were kept.

These heavy objects were lifted by cable and I had argued hard for a swivel arrangement so that the twisting motion inevitable in flight would not place any strain on the hook. My plea was ignored and despite my protests I was instructed to move the gear without the attachment.

The breakup of camp was being filmed by the contractor who had been working the job, as the concluding episode in a picture record of the summer's work. He took pictures as I moved the equipment. It was a good day for film making, as far as weather was concerned.

Quite a bit of the gear was across the lake when I returned for the seismic box. It was secured to the cable and I lifted off, taking great care because of the value of the package.

All seemed to be going normally until we were about 150 feet in the air, when I felt the chopper jump.

I banked the helicopter just in time to spot the box plunging into the trees—with its $65,000 cargo of instruments. They were smashed beyond repair, a complete writeoff. The ring on the cable had twisted out of the hook.

The sidebar to the story was the end of the film record. The cameraman, when he saw the box break loose, dropped the camera and stood in open-mouthed disbelief as the costliest item of camp stores disintegrated.

That was the end of the most expensive helicopter assignment on which I ever worked. It had involved two 'copters, with daily flights from Hay River to Buffalo Lake where we put the 'copters down on the water, attached an outboard motor to the floats and used them as boats for placing dynamite with one machine and measuring the blast on equipment in the second machine. A boat would have been much cheaper but that wasn't our problem.

In addition to the loss of the seismic instruments there had been an earlier mishap in which a metal drill tower had been dropped while in flight and so damaged it had to be flown out to Edmonton for a complete renovation. Insurance companies won't provide coverage for losses of this sort, which illustrates why modern day mining is a high risk venture and why those who indulge in it need to get the occasional big return.

You might say that was the end of my interrupted honeymoon and more than explains why Ingeborg and I felt we would like to settle down quietly in some nice town somewhere.

We decided to become home owners and were entranced by the design planning for a structure due to be completed early in 1964.

It was all very new and exciting, for a few weeks. But flying is about as easy to give up as breathing. Inge soon spotted all the old signs of the grounded airman— moodiness, irritability, restlessness, constant peering up at the sky and wondering about weather conditions.

Just before Christmas, 1963, we had a message from Guy Earle wishing us a Merry Christmas and expressing the hope I would be on the 1964 hunt. I firmly put it aside, physically at least.

Our house was to be finished in February, but not for us. The more I thought and talked about it the more inviting the smelly old seal hunt loomed. Inge agreed it was the thing for me to do. Spartan was willing, and the deal was sealed with an invitation to Inge to go on the seal hunt with me.

By coincidence we decided to abandon Grande Prairie the day the house was finished. A kind neighbor, lawyer Jeff Ouellete, who was astonished at the development, agreed to act as my agent in the sale of the house. We left, never having set foot in our dream castle, and drove to Ottawa across the wintery prairie. I don't know for sure how Inge felt, but I was ecstatic.

We invested some of our money in the parkas, ski pants and heavy underclothing I now knew were a necessity on the North Atlantic in March.

This time I flew my helicopter to the Maritimes with my

engineer as a passenger. Inge joined us at Carbonear where we were in good time to board the **Kyle** before departure. The dull outline of the antiquated former C.P.R. vessel staggered her at first. Married quarters for us turned out to be a cubicle with two bunk beds, a small sink, a midget porthole and barely enough room to turn around in without skinning elbows.

Inge cheered up at sailing time for a large crowd had assembled to wish us *bon voyage*—doubtless a few of them wondered about the first woman they had ever seen go off with the sealing fleet, recalling the ancient marine superstition that it was unlucky to sail with a female aboard.

It had been a long, eventful day so we retired early and, with a touch of male gallantry, I settled any doubt about the occupancy of upper and lower berths by volunteering to sleep upstairs. It was a narrow perch some five feet above the cabin floor, best attained by use of a small ladder. I had fallen into a deep sleep when there was a loud, peremptory knock on the door.

My R.C.A.F. instinct to scramble betrayed me in the half dazed condition of the moment. I stepped off the bunk and found that first step a rather long one as I plunged to the floor of the cabin, severely wrenching my right wrist, injuring my shoulder, and slicing a long gash in my forehead. Inge's first tendency was to laugh until she saw the blood streaming down my face. The message bearer, it turned out, was a member of the crew, still affected by the excitement of leavetaking, who merely wanted to tell me what I already knew—that I would have to get up really early in the morning.

The fall seemed to create a pinched nerve condition in my neck that still bothers me, and throughout the hunt I was forced to operate with badly sprained fingers that made it difficult to grasp the controls.

The captain had the ship's carpenter dismantle the upper berth and reassemble it in line with Inge's. He couldn't afford to hazard any more unnecessary risks to the chopper man.

As usual, Earle was after his share of the harp seal pelts but he also had set his mind on acquiring a few of the magnificent hood seal furs. The hoods are tremendously impressive specimens. They often grow to 13 feet in length and five feet in girth and the skins and fat from such monarchs of the ice weigh as much as 900 pounds per animal.

Unlike the timid harps, the hoods are fearless. Mother harps scurry for safety when the hunters approach, abandoning their young to the raiders by diving through air holes into the safety of the water below the ice. Since the babies cannot swim for several weeks after birth, their fate is certain if they are abandoned.

The hoods are as fearless as the harps are cowardly. The mother hood rises to full height when the hunters appear, baring tusks and ready to fight and die for the safety of her offspring.

A hood aroused is a sight never to be forgotten, one marred for me by memories of seven hunters clubbing down one giant specimen in a sickening spectacle of animal murder.

This second hunt was plagued with difficulties—from the late arrival of the seals to exceptionally extensive and heavy pack ice that taxed the tough old **Kyle's** ability to buck its way through.

The fight to gain the sealing grounds never stopped, as the **Kyle** fought the rafted ice, some of it 16 feet thick. The ship butted into it, engine roaring, like an enraged bull. There were times when, progress halted, the crew ran out on the ice and blasted away the worst of it.

I marvelled at their foolhardy courage for they were using black powder, loosely poured into canisters. Fuses were lit and the explosive mixture dropped through ice cracks or air holes, the blasting crew running off at top speed to evade the dangers created by their uncertain bombs. It was slow, time-consuming, expensive travel, with real danger of damage to the vessel from the ice, as we soon discovered.

As we bulled our way through the pack our radio man picked up an urgent call for help from the modern sealer, the **Sir John Crosby,** a much newer and more handsome vessel than ours. Her skipper messaged that his ship was in trouble, stuck in heavy ice with her forward hold taking water faster than her pumps could remove it.

The law of the sea is stern and those who go upon its waters, or through its ice, refuse a call for help at their peril. Earle dutifully directed the **Kyle** towards the **Crosby,** some 30 miles away and well off the course on which we were proceeding. A few hours later we edged alongside and our emergency pumps began to help clear the forward hold. The next morning the mighty **Sir John A,** moving at the double to help the **Crosby,** arrived. She was placed on a circular ice-smashing course and by the time the **Crosby** was out of danger, had freed both of us from the embrace of the ice floes and we departed on our search north.

It was time to start the hunt and at first light on the morning of March 10 I lifted off on a scouting expedition during which the first mate and I would look for leads, open water passages in the ice, that would permit the **Kyle** to move closer to the hunting grounds.

It was a poor day. A cold, white fog settled in and visibility dropped to about 500 yards. I couldn't see the **Kyle** but I was flying on a carefully plotted compass bearing and felt sure I could return to her whenever I wanted. It was a miscalculation, not entirely my fault, as it turned out.

We flew for about 30 minutes in a northerly direction, the course on which the **Kyle** was proceeding when we took off, but visibility was so poor I decided to return. Making a 180-degree turn, I started back expecting to intercept the **Kyle** 25 miles south.

Unknown to me, while we were flying out the **Kyle** had done a 90-degree turn to port without advising us, so when we came to where the ship should have been there was no sign of her.

We searched in the declining visibility but could not find the **Kyle** and I was beginning to be a bit worried when we came across the **Sir John Crosby.** I landed on the ice beside her and climbed aboard. From her radio room I called the **Kyle** and asked Earle to take a radio fix on us and give us our course, which he did. "Steer zero four five," he told me, "and you'll soon catch up with us."

I took on enough fuel for the short trip and lifted off, being very careful to fly on the bearing given, fully expecting to locate the **Kyle** in 15 minutes or so.

We flew the time I thought was necessary to find the **Kyle** but it was nowhere in sight, the reason being he was away off to port proceeding in a different direction than I had been told.

I was taking no chances. I reversed myself and flew back and was fortunate enough to find once more the **Crosby,** by the grace of God. This time I asked him to take a fix on us and Earle said to steer three-two-zero, a vast difference from zero-four-five. This time I really filled up the tanks for I wanted enough fuel to be able to get to land if I had to. If I didn't find the **Kyle** this time my chance of locating the **Crosby** a third time in the deteriorating conditions was pretty remote.

Earle, it was obvious, hadn't been taking accurate radio bearings on us at all and I wasn't really surprised when we once more couldn't find the **Kyle,** although we flew and flew. It was getting along towards 4:30 in the afternoon but suddenly the visibility cleared and we saw a speck in the ice. "There's the **Kyle,**" I shouted and we headed toward what obviously was a ship.

It was a ship, right enough, but as we drew closer we could see it wasn't the **Kyle,** for it was much smaller than our vessel. But at that point in the day a ship was a ship and it was clear we couldn't fly much longer so we kept right on towards it, and found we had come down on the **Trepassy,** a Newfoundland sealer.

I asked the helicopter engineer where the **Trepassy's** helicopter was and he told me that it had flown on up north scouting for seals and was somewhat overdue, although they had made inquiries by radio earlier and learned that the 'copter had been seen by several other ships in the fleet.

They seemed somewhat more unconcerned than they might have been, in my opinion, and when I had radioed the **Kyle** and informed them I would not hazard leaving the **Trepassy** until the next day, I returned to the subject of the missing craft.

My message to the **Kyle** broke a long period of anxiety for Inge, who was immensely relieved to know I was safe, so much so that when she was told to speak to me on the radio

54

all she could think to say was an old Newfoundland exclamation, "My son, my son, what have you done?" a question that broke up the men on the **Kyle's** bridge.

Back at the **Trepassy** I continued my questioning and found that, despite their 'copter's overdue state, the **Trepassy** hadn't bothered to alert Search and Rescue to the possibility that the helicopter was down somewhere on the frozen sea. I pressed them to act for I felt the lack of concern was getting more than a little ridiculous.

We gave Search and Rescue what little information we had and they quickly got their crews into the air trying to locate the missing chopper and its two occupants. This was a creditable feat of organization as craft were alerted and airborne from Goose Bay in Labrador and Newfoundland's Gander base within about 30 minutes, the R.C.A.F. and the U.S. Air Force combining efforts in the search.

I still wasn't quite sure where the **Kyle** was located and warned Earle, and the ships in our vicinity, that we would fire off a red parachute flare purely for identification, asking Earle to let us know if he could see it.

Both Earle and Inge saw the flare and we went to bed expecting that the **Kyle** would sail towards us and be there next morning by first light.

But Earle, anxious to get to the seals, had other ideas, and kept the **Kyle** pointed in a northerly direction. When I called him up in the morning he was 65 miles away from us, instead of alongside. I thought "That's great," but we had breakfast and took off and after an hour or so spotted the **Kyle**, distinctive with its black smoke plume.

I climbed well up as we approached it, to about 9000 feet, baffling Inge and the crew, for they could hear our motor but could not see us. They were looking for us on a normal low level approach and were stunned when we dropped straight down.

Search and Rescue efforts were continuing with no word of the **Trepassy** pair and their craft. I worked a full day still wondering if they were safe but finally, about seven o'clock that night learned they had been spotted by one of the search planes, down on the ice but safe and only shaken up and chilled.

Search and Rescue realized it was too late to ask for a helicopter pickup so they set up a night patrol with duty planes flying over the site of the downed chopper through the hours of darkness while the icebreaker **Sir Humphrey Gilbert** cruised through the ice to pick them up.

That seemed the end of the episode, but it wasn't. Next morning Search and Rescue radioed to ask the **Kyle** if it could arrange the pickup by air as the **Gilbert,** battling heavy ice, was almost stalled some 11 miles from the downed bird.

We were nearly 80 miles from the spot but Earle agreed and I took off with him and the first mate, with some added weight in the form of a full bottle of Scotch whisky he had tucked in his pocket. An R.C.A.F. Albatross escorted us to the downed crew, who were stiff and cold, a condition that the whisky relieved. Poured onto stomachs that hadn't hosted food for nearly 40 hours, it produced a rapid onset of high spirits so that when I got the two men to the icebreaker the captain was amazed at their hilarity as they staggered along the deck.

The **Gilbert** had been stalled 11 miles from the stranded helicopter from which I had rescued the two men but it got going later and picked up the machine, which otherwise might eventually have gone through the ice and been lost in the depths.

The R.C.A.F. Albatross, still on patrol, shepherded me back to the downed chopper where I had left Earle and the first mate and then on the the **Kyle,** like a mother hen, turning tight circles so that it could stay even with my chopper, bravely doing 60 miles an hour to the 160 mph speed of the Albatross. It was sheepdogging, and it was great, and we loved the air force boys for their professional attention to a very important business.

Of all the service flyers in peace time the Search and Rescue crews do the most satisfying and worthwhile job. They fully earn their rank and privileges and the respect of flyers everywhere.

We were now three days into the hunting season and had yet to locate our first seal, a condition that was sending the morale thermometer down to new daily lows. The sealer has little or nothing to do, or that he wants to do, on a seal hunt, but hunt and sleep. Inge managed to keep a bit busier doing improvised domestic chores like washing out bed linen in the cabin hand basin and drying it on a clothes line strung around those small confines. I guess alone among the 106 men aboard we had clean linen at least once a week.

Finally, on the morning of March 14, our luck turned, for we spotted seals and shouted the happy news back over the radio. We returned to a ship in total commotion, men falling into winter gear and lining up to be flown to the killing ground where they were left, two by two, and ran off to start collecting pelts, while the ship brought in the main body of men.

Inge viewed the scene with fascinated astonishment for everyone was doing something as all raced to make up for lost days. The pelts began to pile up on the ice and I flew non-stop, lifting them from the sealing area and flying them back to the ship, 600 pounds or more in each sling of skins.

I had perfected the delicate art of sweeping in at 50 mph and releasing the load of pelts so they would skid into a flat area on the ice near the ship.

It was precision bombing in a way and required alertness among the members of the ground crew that was not always evident. Inge almost saw a tragedy that day when two of the ship's crew, waiting on the ice to retrieve offloaded pelts to be winched on to the **Kyle,** failed to move quickly enough from the center of the drop area as I came in to unload.

The big, wet pack of skins whizzed between them, brushing one man's arm. It was a near miss. A direct hit could have projected both of them into the side of the ship and probably killed them. I was extremely angry at the carelessness of the ground crew but the story of what had happened got around and there was no more lally-gagging in the drop path.

The eagerness of the sealers to get to work made it particularly important for me to warn each pair of them to keep their 10-foot poles free of the helicopter rotors. I made them carry their poles at the trail in the vicinity of the aircraft which imposed a few seconds delay in their attack on the seal pups but gave me a chance to take off without having to watch the slaughter, something I never did get used to in two seasons.

The sealers worked from dawn to dusk, eating lunch sandwiches with one hand and poling down seals with the other as they munched. It was a primitive scenario but nothing seemed to spoil their appetite either for the hasty, indifferent lunches they carried or the sight of the bloody, but highly rewarding pelts.

The sealers were a rough crowd, but Inge and I found them to be unfailingly courteous, polite, cheerful but restrained in her presence.

We were fortunate to collect 8000 pelts in that indifferent sealing year for good luck was a necessity, as well as good management. Some ships were not so fortunate and at least one, the **Arctic Endeavour,** lost its best hope of winning a share of the scanty harvest when its helicopter crashed.

The chopper crashed about 100 yards from the ship when a net, used to lift pelts, caught on an ice hummock on takeoff, and flipped the machine over on its back.

The pilot was relatively inexperienced and was using the net on a long steel cable. When he started to lift off he was probably 20 or 30 feet in the air with the cable and net dangling below him out of sight. He had no way of knowing for sure that it was clear of the ice hummocks and in this case it caught on some projecting ice.

The unfortunate pilot had compound fractures of his left leg and arm, a severe bash on the skull, and his back was injured. He was conscious but in severe pain. The crew from the ship and his engineer managed to get him out of the cabin of the helicopter which, fortunately, did not catch on fire. By the time the injured man had been carried on to the ship he was writhing in agony. To make him settle down he was given a shot of morphine, the only tranquilizer they had in the medicine chest. It was then around 5 p.m.

They immediately alerted the **Sir John A. Macdonald** and the ship's captain promptly set a course for the **Arctic Endeavour.** It was some distance away but the big ship pulled alongside about three o'clock in the morning, a considerable feat of navigation, having pounded its way through 11 feet of ice at full bore.

In the meantime, the **Endeavour** captain had talked with a doctor in the hospital at St. Anthony, about 65 miles away, who mentioned that if the pilot had suffered severe head injuries he should in no circumstance be given a shot of morphine, for it might be fatal.

Informed by the injured man's shocked attendants that this had already been done, the doctor told them they could only hope it would come out all right.

The stricken pilot was transferred to the **Sir John A.** which immediately began to move off in the direction of St. Anthony. At first light the patient was loaded aboard the ship's helicopter and flown the rest of the way.

For a time his condition was critical and they even flew out his wife to be with him from Montreal. He recovered after about six months and eventually returned to flying. I believe he even went back on the seal hunt the next year.

The footnote to the story is the unbelievable fact that the damaged helicopter, which might easily have been lifted on to the deck of the ship, was abandoned on the ice, depsite the $50,000 or more it was worth as repairable salvage.

The **Kyle** passed it by as we all thought the **Arctic Endeavour** would be coming back to get it. Had we known it would not, we could have taken it as salvage.

It was probably my one best chance to become the owner of my own private helicopter, and I muffed it. Instead it seems to have sunk through the melting ice to join the great fleet of mixed craft Davey Jones has been accumulating on the sea bottom.

We had the best day of that indifferent season on March 19 when in a position roughly 30 miles off the coast of Labrador we sighted a seal patch of some 6000 animals. Seven other ships raced us to the spot but we made off with 1200 pelts that day, more than our share.

Perhaps 'made off' is not the best phrasing for it has other meanings in the seal hunt. Some pelts are 'made off with' by people who didn't take the furs in the first place.

This hijacking opportunity was created by the practice of hunters piling their pelts in heaps and marking them with special flags indicating the ownership of the pile. In a busy season the retrieval of the pelts often would not take place for some time after the sealers had moved on to other parts of the hunting grounds.

Hours, even days, could pass before their ship came close enough to lift the pelts, or the helicopters could move them, as I learned to do. With the movement of ice there were times when floes would get completely away and the pelts be left alone, perhaps miles from the owners.

The practice is to lift these pelt piles regardless of the flags, but for the most part the hijacking was not planned or organized, although in one case a group from Montreal was cught with stolen furs and appropriately punished.

On my final flight of a weary day I snatched a baby seal from the slaughterhouse and took it back to Inge, whose delight has to be imagined. She stroked its silky fur. The big saucer eyes looked up at us and we grew weak at the knees and I felt sick at the stomach to think of what was happening to its brothers and sisters.

We both wished so much that we could keep it, an impossible dream, for there was no room and little sentiment for a live animal whose fur would turn spotted and become valueless in a few days. We surrendered it reluctantly. The hunt swallowed it up, along with all the others, and we both felt terribly distressed.

Our good fortune had come to an end. For a week the ice locked us tight and our struggle to get free resulted in the breaking of one of the blades on our three-bladed propeller. After that its revolutions gave the ship an odd skipping motion. The balance was gone but the sturdy, stubborn **Kyle** ploughed on in a fruitless hunt for seals.

Our captain amused himself and amazed us with daily exhibitions of marksmanship, picking off the infrequent seal that turned up at long range. We were moving very slowly, or not at all, so that hunters had plenty of time to leap on to the ice and return with the skin.

Skinning the seals was a brutal business despite all the talk you may hear to the contrary that they are killed before their pelts are removed. In the regular hunt the 10-foot poles rarely killed even the baby seals and I saw many that were still quivering with life and returning consciousness as their pelts were torn from them. Today the hunters are said to use smaller, heavier, more lethal clubs. I can only hope they provide a more merciful finish than the poles did.

After six days of icelocked frustration we spotted some seals and our captain got us released by guile, as I have previously recounted. By this time Inge was cabin-happy and anxious to get off the ship, so on March 23 I took her and the first mate on a sight-seeing, scouting trip.

She proved a good luck charm for eight miles from the **Kyle** she spotted a colony of a couple of thousand seals, and there wasn't another ship in sight.

We alerted the **Kyle** and stooged around before returning to pick up the hunters. It was still cold, the landscape as desolate as ever with no sign of human habitation, which convinced me it was a safe spot to set down on while we retreated to some convenient hummocks to answer the call of nature. Inge went off by herself but returned in haste, as the sound of engines close at hand were heard.

Over and through the hummocks came two snowmobiles driven by smiling natives. They had been hidden behind some mounds of ice and we had failed to see them. When they noted our descent they hurried to see if we were in trouble and if they could help us. They were right, of course, but it wasn't the kind of difficulty they had imagined!

Back at the **Kyle** that night the cook produly prepared a dinner of seal flippers, a Newfoundland delicacy that delighted everyone on board except the bird man and his wife. I've tried them and though I like to think I have few food inhibitions, I simply can't abide seal flippers. They have an inescapable seal oil taste and smell. Inge took one sniff and a small peek and ordered boiled eggs. She said they reminded her of cooked hands.

Seals are edible and more than flippers can be consumed by hungry people. When there is no danger of them spoiling before being eaten, hunters will toss one or two carcasses aboard to consume back home. On the docks they sold for $3 each, while the flippers went like in-store bargains at $1 each. We had brought back about $10,000 worth.

By this time it was obvious the hunt was over although the calendar said there were several more days to go. The ice was thinner and seals scarcer than ever. Earle turned his limping vessel south and headed for home port. Towards evening the sky darkened and we saw what can happen to sealers and why men die in pursuit of the white pelts of the seal pups. One of our sealers, making his way back to the ship toward dusk, suddenly was marooned on a small cake of ice that snapped from the main pack and moved off into open water churned up by the ship's straining propeller.

His danger was obvious. Any movement might further divide the small floe which was only about eight feet across. Sudden movement could upset it, plunging him into Arctic waters in which a man can live only a few minutes and in which it is best to die quickly.

To rescue him Earle had to turn the 250-foot Kyle in the narrow open waters without upsetting the ice island. And he did just that, so skillfully that I marvelled. It took several hours and darkness fell quickly, making it necessary for the **Kyle's** crew to focus blinding spotlights on the small, stricken but courageous figure. The sealer, afraid of slipping in his boots, removed them and stood gallantly in his stocking feet, exchanging talk and jests with his mates, who shouted words of encouragement, advice and ribald speculation of how they would celebrate his rescue if they pulled it off. It was more than two hours before the **Kyle** could inch its way close enough for its crew to throw their endangered mate a rope that snatched him from the horrible death that had been nudging his elbow.

I watched the drama transfixed. I was aware how quickly the ice could betray, for it had almost trapped me earlier in the hunt. That incident had stemmed from one of the sealers having released the emergency handle on the helicopter door as he alighted from the craft. I had warned the men constantly not to touch the door release because if they used the wrong handle the whole door would fall off. And that is what happened.

The sealer was apologetic but too anxious to start hunting to offer to help replace the door.

That left me alone, standing on the helicopter float, trying to hold the metal door in place with one hand while I reset the emergency locking device on the inside of the frame with the other.

It was a difficult job under the best of circumstances and doubly so out on the cold ice. I had almost completed the task when I noticed that the ice pack had split between the floats and that one of them was perilously close to falling into the water, a disaster that would have thrown the main rotors on the ice and probably would have tossed me into the drink. I think I set a record for climbing into the cabin and lifting off, and none too soon.

The sealer's narrow escape from death sparked a festive atmosphere on the ship and our return journey was a happy one despite the small catch. Incidents such as this explain why I admire the rugged men of the outports, sturdy Canadians who mix cruelty with gentleness and courage, individuals of serious mien but unfailing good humor, qualities that make them unique among Canadians, in my estimation.

Due to improper diet, their distance from dentists, and low family incomes that inhibit expenditure of dental care, many Newfoundlanders, particularly those of the older generations, have poor teeth. It is an affliction they bear with rare good humor, as they do so many other things that make life difficult foi them on those rugged shores.

This condition makes a row of smiling Newfoundlanders at the dining table resemble a group photo of a modern hockey team with their store teeth removed. It makes for difficult chewing, too. One night we had steak for dinner. It was a bit tough, so much so that one of the crew, whose front teeth were conspicuous by their absence, asked for a toothpick. A friend slipped from the dining area and returned with a hunk of two-by-four as the diners exploded with mirth, in which the toothless one joined.

We docked at Carbonear on April 3. News of our return had preceded us and as we sailed in at seven o'clock in the evening I'll swear every living soul in town was there to greet us. Ships' horns—whistles—bells and flares—glowed in the sky as we docked—a real home-coming.

Inge and I wouldn't have missed that seal hunt for anything, but as we hurried to the hotel, to the joy of a hot bath with unlimited amounts of water and soap, we both realized, with a deep pang of regret, that it was an experience we should never repeat.

Not everyone on the **Kyle** shared our rush to get ashore. Four days later I was surprised to learn that three men were still aboard the vessel: the first mate, the steward and the engineer. The last two had some official reason to stay for they had clearing up duties to perform, but the presence of the first mate baffled me until I talked with Gordie, the steward. "Him," Gordie said, "Hell, he's so damn cheap he wouldn't pay 50 cents to see Christ walk on water." It was cheaper to live aboard than go ashore.

I have my own views about the seal hunt. Many aspects of it revolted me and left my physically ill, but I do not subscribe to the notion that the hunt should be stopped. The argument for that is equally applicable to halting the operation of abattoirs.

I can accept the view that seal pelts are a natural resource, one to be utilized and properly controlled. As it has so many other things, nature has provided a plentitude of seals for the use of man. They are not only clothing but, even in modern times, food and income for the residents of the outports.

Primitive man first took the seals because of a need to sustain life. The criterion today has been greed, heedless of appalling waste, inhuman hunting methods and a callousness that irritated me. Nature's food chain provides life and death but the various sub-human life forms arrange it so that nothing, in the end, is wasted. Only 'the highest life form' has been able to devise that, in the seal hunt almost everything has been wasted.

The hunt should be controlled by international agreement, strictly enforced, that will permit the seals not only to survive but to flourish. And I would make it obligatory to kill them in a much more humane fashion than by clubbing.

A rifle shot would be quickest and surest but the use of firearms on ice floes, where ricochets could endanger hunters, is obvious. Why not some kind of high-powered air pistol, placed at the head of the quarry, for the seal seldom tries to escape and could not do so if it tried. Stockyard animals destined for table meat are quickly slain. We can, at least, do as much for the seals.

Beyond that, there should be total utilization of the resource through the processing of the entire carcass, something only the Russians manage to achieve. For there need be no waste and total utilization would give some justification for the slaughter of these harmless animals.

Having said that, I must take issue with those who oppose the seal hunt on the terms of the Greenpeace Foundation. Their effort to prevent the taking of the baby seals descended from the sublime to the ridiculous and put them in the position of accepting the double standard that it is proper for Canadians to hunt seals but immoral for Norwegians and other foreigners to do the same.

Though I agree with some of their motivation it is sad to think that they had to travel 4000 miles to find out the facts of economic life in the outports of Newfoundland.

As anyone who had first-hand knowledge of the seal hunt must have known, they were wasting their time and effort and the few seals they may have protected won't have amounted to anything. Newfoundland families which rely on seals for one-third of their income rightly resented this attempt by ignorant outsiders to steal the bread out of their mouths. As I knew would be the case, few helicopter pilots were willing to risk losing their licences to ferry the protesters across the wide expanse of the hunt area. It is nonsense to talk about living on the ice, and the physical job of finding the seals, in an area up to 80 miles in extent and 40 miles wide, seems not to have been realized by the Greenpeace group.

They are paying the penalties of ignorance by loss of moral prestige. They compromised; and whether you agree with them or not, that is the last thing most people expected they would do.

Our Newfoundland experience continued after the seal hunt until the end of 1964, giving Inge and me an opportunity to get better acquainted with the country and the truly fine people who inhabit it.

After a brief spell relieving a helicopter pilot on the Bechtel corporation power project at Twin Falls, Labrador, I moved back to the west coast of Newfoundland supporting a prospecting party of Leach Gold Mine people headed by Charlie Pegg, a veteran prospector and mining man. Other members of the group included his two lieutenants, Ivan Watson and Bill Smitheringale, both experienced geologists. There were about 10 in the main party plus additional crews of local people hired on the site.

The target of the search was primarily zinc and lead, but like prospectors the world over, the searchers were prepared to deal with anything they might find in the way of marketable minerals. The standard operational method included the transportation of teams of two to places in the bush where they would set up camp and conduct a daily area search, on foot, for mineral traces. Every five or six days I would fly them in to new areas.

After putting down the teams of locals I would fly out Pegg, Watson and Smitheringale, the professional geologists, who would do their own prospecting. It was an efficient operation from my standpoint although I cannot begin to judge it in the terms of mineral exploration and really knew little or nothing of what was being discovered, for mining men are notoriously close-mouthed.

It was the first time I ever had 'office hours' in the chopper field for I worked from eight in the morning to five in the afternoon. The best part of it was that the Newfoundland assignment permitted Inge to join me at the field headquarters. I was only in the air two or three hours a day (I wasn't required for scouting) so I spent a good deal of time at the base we had set up at Portland Creek.

Pegg would have liked it to be otherwise. The first time I flew him into the bush he asked me to wait. I thought he would only be a couple of hours but he stayed away until late afternoon while I sat sweltering in the 'copter cabin. It was impossible to go outside because of the flies and mosquitos and when the cabin was closed to keep them out the temperature almost fried me.

When Pegg returned I told him that I would not be able to spend the whole day waiting for him at whatever point I had put him down. Charlie argued but I insisted. We were only 15 or 20 miles from camp and it made no sense to be isolated in the wilderness. Leach provided bunkhouse quarters at a sort of motel at Portland Creek and the whole crew stayed in them.

Inge and I required separate quarters which we had to pay for ourselves. We talked it over and decided that for our next move we would try living in a tent so we drove down to Cornerbrook and bought a 12x18-foot, two-room tent with zipper doors in the walls. We fitted it out with a three-quarter size bed, tables and chairs, two Coleman stoves and three Coleman lamps, everything down to our own little commode biffy.

The first place we set up housekeeping in our tent was at Flowers Cove where we selected a site on a bluff overlooking the sea beside the Harborview Hotel, a typical 2½-storey Newfoundland wooden house tenanted by a man, his wife and daughter, who rented out rooms as opportunity afforded.

It wasn't long before we found out that the scenic beauty of our site hardly matched the disadvantages of constant high winds that threatened to blow us into the ocean. Within a few days we struck our tent and set it up in a sheltered area closer to the center of the outpost, next to a vacant house that gave us some added protection.

There were quite a few houses to rent in Newfoundland wherever we went, some of them seemingly abandoned on short notice by islanders trekking to greener pastures.

Life in a tent wasn't bad although it had its drawbacks. I used to alert Inge when I returned by hovering close to our camp site, whereupon she would get dinner ready for us. One day I gave the usual signal, set the machine down, did my usual log book updating and other office chores, then headed for home in good appetite. This time the dinner wasn't ready and I found Inge in a state of high agitation and our tent in high disorder.

I was lucky not to find worse than that. When Inge filled the stove and the lamps that morning, a daily task, she had left a valve open on the stove, permitting a leakage of fuel that leaped into flame as she attempted to light the stove, which was in the back room of the tent.

Reacting instinctively, she grabbed the blazing stove, got through two of those zippered doors and hurled it out onto the ground. She might have been burned to death before anyone could have helped but she escaped without harm. She said her first fear had been that our lovely tent would be destroyed. I told her never to worry about that: tents, at least, are replaceable. Inges are not.

It was a grand summer, though, giving us full opportunity to indulge our taste for fresh sea food. Trips to the dock were rewarded with delicious lobster, cod and other sea creatures caught only a few miles away, and at prices that left us gasping. On one occasion I bought the whole catch of lobsters from one fisherman, 40 pounds of them, for 50 cents a pound. What we couldn't eat fresh Inge canned. They were superb either way.

People who think cod is food for the poor ought to try it fresh from the ocean, cut in thick fillets, and either deep fried, fried in butter or barbecued. Canadians just don't understand how good fish can be or they would eat more of it than they do.

Not only the coastal waters provided gourmet food. The summer nights offer long hours of daylight in Newfoundland and work ended at five o'clock. Charlie never wanted the helicopter at night. Frequently Inge and I would take off for fishing on a couple of small lakes about 15 miles from camp. They were too small for visitations by float planes and almost inaccessible to a fisherman on foot. They swarmed with trout, which moved from one lake to the other through a small connecting river. Honestly, you could catch a fish on every cast and there was seldom a minute when they weren't taking a lure.

It wasn't sport in the grand style. That kind of fishing calls for lengthy, skilled stalking of the finny victim. These plump **pisces** needed no such coaxing. I would frequently put on two hooks and reel in with two fish on the single line.

We kept nothing under a foot and threw back far more than we kept. It was obvious to us that no one else ever fished those lakes.

One day we decided to share these delights with our hotel owner friend and caught some four dozen trout for his dining room. Everyone ate trout for dinner the next night, oohing and aahing about them. We did, too, for they were skillfully prepared and served, but our delight vanished when I was presented with a bill for dinner although I had fed everyone in the hotel. The proprietor, a man named Wentzel, was a canny man with a buck but I finally persuaded him that he ought not to grudge a few grains to the ox that had trod out the corn.

During our stay in the area Inge and I celebrated our second wedding anniversary, an occasion that led us to put on a party. I bought seven bottles of whisky from Wentzel for the occasion. He billed me $7.00 each for corkage, for whisky I am reasonably certain he obtained free of taxes from visiting ships where it cost him only about $1.50 a bottle.

Canadians in other parts of the country probably have the idea that Newfoundlanders are simple people, usually in the worst sense of the word, a notion I'm sure is propagated by the islanders themselves who very likely have an official Newfie joke author creating humorous slander for them to distribute to reinforce the thought. In my experience the smartest can wheel-and-deal with the best around, and I guess they get a good deal of fun out of misleading the ignorant from Upper Canada.

For example, I noticed that the whisky bottle in the hotel bar never seemed to get empty, although the label on it was a bit worn and stained. I became convinced it was the same bottle, one without a bottom. One night I slyly marked the whisky height with a pencil when the bar closed. It was a label of an expensive Canadian brand. The next night it was back, full and still stained. Obviously it was being refilled when necessary although I wouldn't swear to what the replacement spirits were, or from where they had come.

Flowers Cove was near the Straits of Belle Isle, a region where the geographical features and the conjunction of air currents combined to provide a wind tunnel effect that equals anything I have ever experienced. It not only made the handling of the helicopter difficult but it drew heavily on fuel and reduced cruising range as a result. One day, having been buffeted by the gales, I found myself almost out of gas and clearly unable to get back to camp. I put the chopper down beside the only road in that part of the island and waited until a south-bound motorist came along. I asked him to stop in Flowers Cove and notify my engineer, Ray Couersol, what had happened to me.

An hour or so later Ray drove up in the company jeep, accompanied by my wife, with a load of gasoline which I poured into the chopper tank. I lifted off in the teeth of a rising gale and after some coaxing, my machine, a few hundred feet up, showed an air speed of 70 mph. Ray had promised to stay nearby and the jeep was crawling along the road at what I found out later was a mere 10 mph, and it was keeping right up with the 'copter.

It was a good summer despite one or two bouts of irritation that arise in remote areas where, after a while, people get on one anothers nerves merely because they are isolated. We had our moments, one of them when Charlie Pegg, some two hours late, failed to appear for a rendezvous. I flew a search pattern, returned to the pickup spot and could not find him. Becoming alarmed, for I had stressed promptness both on the part of the passenger and of myself, I flew back to camp, grabbed a medical kit and took Bill Smitheringale along, worried that some accident had befallen even as experienced an outdoor man as Charlie. This time he was ready at the rendezvous, incensed because I hadn't been waiting for him despite his being long overdue.

On another occasion I had a run-in with Ivan Watson who returned to camp in the late afternoon and learned that I had not gone out to pick up the teams set down earlier that day. It was a decision I had taken reluctantly, forced on me when a tremendous wind arose. It would mean a night in the bush for those who elected not to walk out to the road, something any of them could have done, but they would be unlikely to suffer much discomfort as each party was outfitted with a tent, ample food for several days and other supplies such as fishing gear, in case of such emergencies.

Ivan had been some 50 miles to the south and sniffed that he hadn't noticed any high winds in that area, which was very likely true for they frequently were regional in scope, growing with intensity as you neared the straits.

A helicopter pilot, like an airplane pilot and a ship's captain, is the sole judge of the performance of his command ship, whether it sails or flies, and how people behave in it, points I was quick to make. It is not an area in which decisions are made by a camp meeting vote, and, I trust, never will be. Ivan might have considered that I was saving the company money because they were paying on an hourly-use basis in the air as well as through a monthly retainer.

I guess one of the things that riled me was the implication that I was 'goofing off'. I suggested that if he wasn't satisfied with me and the service provided he ought to get me replaced and urged him to telephone Ottawa with the suggestion. It was the last I heard of it, and there was no more trouble in the decision-making process of when I should be airborne.

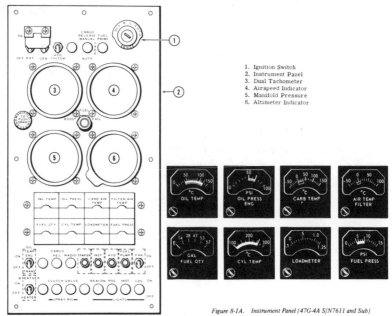

1. Ignition Switch
2. Instrument Panel
3. Dual Tachometer
4. Airspeed Indicator
5. Manifold Pressure
6. Altimeter Indicator

*Figure 8-1A. Instrument Panel (47G-4A S/N7611 and Sub)*

# 5

# Lost Is a Nasty Word

No aircraft pilot, unless he has been tried, convicted and saved by Search and Rescue, is likely to concede that he ever got lost.

The operative words are 'unsure of my position', and more than a few of us have been that way placed.

Sometimes, of course, those words are the truth, but a good many flyers have been temporarily lost in situations they prefer to describe as a mere uncertainty of location. It happens very early in the careers of some, among whom I can be numbered, but very seldom thereafter if they have any flair for the business.

Two of us, experienced flyers at that, got lost on the same day early in my career with Okanagan and we were more than a little fortunate to be able to elude all the penalties that can be imposed on a lost flyer, dangers we managed to avoid through a set of fortuitous circumstances to which we made little or no contribution.

Laymen are likely to understand how difficult it is to fly by visual sighting across miles of white ice and snow. They may find it more difficult to appreciate how a pilot can get lost in mountainous country where peaks, valleys and rivers form a distinctive pattern.

In fact, it probably is easier to get lost in the mountains than almost anywhere for there is an excess of landmarks.

Many of them look alike from several thousand feet in the air and more so at closer range, and for the most part helicopters fly at low altitudes.

One flat-top mountain is much the same as another, and one river bend is a twin for another. Forests? They all look alike.

Along the spiny mountain backbone of the western half of the North American continent the mountain chains have a fair share of eminences that have no peak because their tops were blown off ages ago by volcanic action. One pointed peak with snow on its flanks resembles another, and among the thousands of them in the long chain there are hundreds of look-alikes in a single region.

So perhaps it was no wonder that Jim Grady and I got into trouble only a few score miles from our destination at Syd Lake, where this story began in the first chapter.

We took command of a pair of choppers in Vancouver on assignment with Standard Oil Co. of California, and were to fly them 2175 miles from Vancouver to the Yukon camps. It wasn't crows'-flight flying, which is why the mileage mounted. We were short-hopping, stopping to work several weeks en route. Jim's destination, in fact, was a second camp 65 miles beyond Syd Lake, but we proposed to fly in tandem for company and safety in case one went down with engine or other problems. The final legs of our trip were to be from Whitehorse to Dawson to Syd Lake and beyond.

I had my engineer Bert Fallman in the cockpit, a man with 250 hours of pilot experience on fixed wing craft, whom I thought would be able to help me navigate. We left Vancouver on May 14, heading in stages to Summit Lake at Mile 392 on the Alaska Highway where we had some work to do for our party of five prospecting geologists. We short-hopped via Prince George, Fort St. John and Fort Nelson, having to hole up in the last-named spot for three days because of bad weather.

Summit was no picnic. We could find no place to make camp and had to settle for a dry river bed, anchoring the tent ropes with rocks because we couldn't drive the pegs into the stony river bottom. About the second night we were there a terrific wind came up about two o'clock in the morning and all of us found our tents collapsed over us and half the camp being blown away in the darkness.

We got that sorted out and worked the area for about 10 days, my first job with the geologists with whom I was to be associated that summer. Our camp was about 4000 feet above sea level in rugged country that provided me with plenty of opportunity to put into practice all the theory I had been absorbing about wilderness flying, things like revving up and leaping the chopper off steep cliffs to get airborne. It was a real grind for our normally aspirated engine, for frequently we were working 8500 or 9000 feet up.

On 31 May we arrived at Whitehorse, capital of the Yukon Territory, and laid over there for a couple of days. On one of them, a Saturday, when I might have been doing some sightseeing, I found myself helping Bert give my helicopter a thorough cleaning. He had only been doing normal maintenance at Summit, changing oil, fueling and other minor duties, but the machine hadn't been kept clean the way a chopper needs to be. Bert wasn't really attuned to bush flying and possibly didn't realize the necessity for a spotlessly shining vehicle in the rough country.

Regardless of where it is being operated a 'copter needs to be kept spotless for a variety of reasons, the most important being safety. When you do a daily inspection it is vital to detect any cracks or flaws in the tubing. A dirty machine gets covered with a patina of oil and dust that can cover such defects. If you miss the flaws one of them could put an end to your career.

After spending all day working on the machine, cleaning down with varsol and elbow grease, a slow burn under which I had been working grew into a bright flame and led me to remind Bert that daily maintenance at this level was his job and would be so in the future. It was a hell of a way to spend a rest period. Engineers can rest when the pilot is airborne.

We took off once more and about 20 minutes down the river came to an island on which we could see another fuel dump, much larger than the first.

We put down beside it and discovered it was 3,000 gallons of company fuel, properly stacked and stamped, apparently set down for summer work. These caches, I was to find, are put out in the winter, carried in by ski-equipped planes. Clearly we were in territory that had to be within the orbit of the summer working schedule of our employers. The miracle was that we had stumbled on it when we might so easily have hared off down some other watercourse and found nothing.

It was really fantastic for we now had enough fuel to keep us airborne all summer. We filled up once more and started down the river. Within a short time we reached a junction with another river that ran off to the south. I turned down that way, for I had a strong feeling we were to the north of Syd Lake. After another 10 min. of flying we saw several old log cabins. By this time food was very much on our minds and we recalled that often, by northern custom, stores of food were left in cabins to assist people in distress. We weren't quite in that category as far as travel was concerned but we might just need all the food we could carry.

I put the machine down beside the huts and we were busy searching them when we both exclaimed that we had heard sounds like those of a helicopter revving up for takeoff.

My first thought was, "It must be Jim looking for us". We ran outside. The noise was continuing although we could see nothing. It obviously was fairly close. I shouted to Bert to stand where he was and keep an eye out for the other chopper. I ran towards ours, leaped in and started the motor. I thought it might be Grady but I really didn't care who it was for anyone in another machine sounded like civilization to me.

As I hurriedly warmed up the motor and prepared to lift off Bert began to wave frantically for me to stay put. It dropped down almost beside me and I could see it was Jim Grady right enough, and thought, "At last we've been found".

I got out and walked over to Grady, grinning rather red-faced as I told him, "Glad to see you, old buddy, for I don't know where in hell we are".

He looked startled and his smile was equally strained. "I don't know where we are, either," he replied. "I thought you were out looking for us".

Jim's plight was worse than ours. He was down to his last spoonful of fuel and had been forced to leave his engineer behind on the bank of the river when he started out to join us because his fuel was so low he needed as little weight as possible, and he wasn't even sure he wouldn't crash in the half-mile he had to fly to meet us.

Jim confessed that he had been flying along another river to the south of us, had gotten completely lost and unable to chart his position.

As I had been, he had been a little cocksure. But we had some sort of excuse for we found later we had flown right off the map sheets they had given us for the flight.

News of the fuel caches heartened him and we decided to bring the whole party together near the log huts. I siphoned off about five gallons of gas so that Jim could fly back and return with his engineer.

He did so and we huddled to consider our next course of action, deciding to fuel up both machines before doing anything else. I took Jim along with me in my chopper to pick up fuel cans, enough to more than top off his and leave us a margin of additional gasoline. As we flew along to the big cache we compared mental notes and came to the conclusion that we were north of Syd Lake and the right thing to do was to follow the southbound river.

Our conviction that this was the answer was so strong that we decided to start the hunt without returning, for the moment at least, to the engineers and the other chopper.

Little more than 30 minutes later we found ourselves approaching a camp close to what was obviously a helicopter pad. As we came down a man sauntered out, ready to greet us. "Where in hell are we?" were our first words. He laughed, took us by an arm and led us into the tent. He pointed out his position on the map. It was about 65 miles north and east of Syd Lake, as we had suspected. How we had reached the spot still baffles me.

It was now about noon. We were an hour's flight from our base so we decided to fly to Syd Lake and let them know we were safe before they alerted Air Rescue and put those obliging people to a lot of unnecessary bother.

It all worked as smoothly as we could have wished. When we set down at Syd Lake we were surprised, and even a little chagrined, to find everything tranquil. "We hadn't been expecting you boys for another couple of days," they told us.

We gassed up and flew back to the engineers, neither of whom could operate the stranded chopper. They were becoming more than distracted by our lengthening absence and were faced with the possibility that we might have crashed and that they might not be found for days or weeks—a thought that set them to firing off distress flares at distant fixed-wing craft that, fortunately, never saw any of them.

Our flight plan from Whitehorse to Dawson City took us by way of Minto where we planned to refuel on some 87-octane previously ordered for delivery there from the White Pass and Yukon transportation people. We couldn't make Dawson in a single hop and Minto looked to be the most reasonable place to break the journey.

Fortunately for our flight schedule, something kept nagging me before we left Whitehorse so I telephoned to make certain the fuel had been delivered at Minto, and found that while it had been taken there the truck driver had returned with it because he couldn't find anyone to sign for it!

Like every problem I got that one sorted out and somewhat more quickly than I might have been able to do if we had flown to Minto before asking questions that could only be answered in Whitehorse.

Grady and I, and our engineers, slept overnight in Dawson, the decaying capital of the long-ago, never-to-be-forgotten gold rush. We had no occasion to linger and arrived at the airport for an early morning takeoff for Syd Lake. It all seemed routine enough, although we were to fly over totally foreign terrain. We had been provided with bluey-white aerial maps, the only ones available in those days. They lacked contour lines, had no color indication of heights and showed only spot heights of a few of the taller mountains. The rivers, critical for navigation as we had to identify and follow several en route, were shown as thin, blue lines.

It was my first experience with maps of this sort, and Bert's as well, but I assumed that he would be able to map

78

read efficiently because of his air experience so I gave him the chore of impromptu navigator and map reader for our 125-mile journey. We flew along quite happily for some time. I felt Bert knew what he was doing and heard and saw nothing to indicate otherwise. We planned to use the Peel River for the final leg of the trip and were keeping a sharp lookout for that landmark.

After what seemed to have become a considerable period of flight time I asked Bert to show me where we were, and suddenly realized he was unsure of our position—there's that phrase again.

Under questioning it came up much worse. Bert said he hadn't the slightest notion of our position. I realized that he had been too embarrassed to say so, although it would have been much easier to repair our error if he had spoken up as soon as he realized he was uncertain.

In many subsequent years of flying I have let my engineer, and others, map read for me but I have kept a close eye, ever since, on the map board, asking frequently for a position indication on the map to confirm my own reading. That was one useful lesson of this 1958 experience, one bought at a high risk cost.

Anyway, we were somewhere north and east of Dawson, and I felt that on elapsed time we really should have reached Syd Lake, so I landed because the gas gauge was showing a little empty and I never trust those devices anyway. The dip stick proved we had about 30 minutes fuel left, not nearly enough to return to Dawson even if we knew the shortest way back. There was a very real problem of what to do. A flyer's first feeling is to stay put. Bert and I talked it over and I made a big decision.

"We'll fly for 20 min.," I said, "and if we haven't come across Syd Lake in that time we'll land and just sit it out. That way we'll have some gas to light signal fires if we need them."

I warned Bert to keep a sharp lookout for any signs of human habitation, which we might hope to find along some river bank. Off we flew and, unbelievably, within seven or eight minutes I spotted some newish-looking wooden cases stacked on the starboard bank of a river.

To our amazement and delight, upon examination after we had set down beside them, we found they contained about 120 gallons of 87-octane in California Standard boxes, two five-gallon tins to the box. No one could be seen and it was obvious they had been placed there some time earlier.

I topped off our fuel tanks from my employer's cache but before we lifted off I penned a note and stuck it to one of the boxes. It gave our names, the date, and the course on which we were proceeding. At least if we were forced down again someone, eventually, would have some idea of where we had been headed.

Pushing it to the limit we had a flight range of 2 hrs., 15 min., so I told Bert we would fly down that unknown river on which we had found the providential fuel cache for 40 or 45 minutes. If we hadn't found anything or anyone in that time we would return to the cache.

My plan was then to load up the chopper with all the fuel we could carry and head southwest to intercept the Alaska highway somewhere east of Whitehorse.

My log shows that the trip was one of my longest for it took 9 hrs., 25 min. to cover what should have been a 125-mile excursion. I can't honestly say that the slowness of the trip ever really distressed me. It might have taken a great deal longer—something like forever, even.

The law of the North holds that it is right and proper to use caches when they are needed. It suggests that real men only use as much as they need, carefully put away the remainder, and at some future time try to replace the supplies if possible. I have no doubt that in fuel caches the user sometimes pays for the gasoline if he can't replace it.

It's a good law, a gentleman's agreement that most respect. A few break it. I had a 140-gallon fuel cache stolen on a northern job, arriving to find a bare five gallons left of a stock on which my working schedule depended.

But that's a rare occurrence. The rule-breaker is not only a thief but he is risking a life. If his example persuades many to follow his precepts there might just be a day when the life at hazard will be his.

# 6

# A Slight Cry of Wolf

Invariably, when the talk turns to life on the frontier, someone wants to know about all the dangers people face from wild animals. Top of the list is questioning about wolves—proving that the late Jim Curran of Sault Ste. Marie persuaded no one at all with his dictum that "any man who sez he was et by a wolf is a damn liar".

People still believe wolves will attack humans. A few probably suspect that there is nothing a wolf enjoys for lunch more than a meaty leg from some unfortunate traveller. It seems to be an inherited state of mind, hyped up by old drawings and paintings of remarkable and imaginary incidents like that famous picture of the Russians in the troika beset by wolves, and the accompanying story of how they tossed people to the wolf pack to permit the survivors to escape. Those wolves were the Siberian species, large enough to devour a horse in a couple of gulps: Hence the phrase 'tossed to the wolves'. Even today some children are told about Little Red Riding Hood, the near-victim of a tricky wolf who had previously dined handsomely on the child's unwary grandmother.

It's all pretty much of a piece. My evidence has to be that I could count the number of wolves I have seen in their habitat, on the legs of a piano stool. The closest I ever came to one was examining the carcass of a deceased *Lupus,* an unfortunate animal despatched by some overenthusiastic campers who thought there was a bounty on such vermin. Their disappointment when they found out the bounty law didn't hold in the Yukon was intense.

While I hold no stock in the wolf-eats-man theory I must confess that it is a spine-chilling, goosebump-raising experience to sit in your tent on the edge of some northern lake and hear the wolves keening their laments down the night air. You would swear they had the camp surrounded and under siege and only something vitally important, like a response to an urgent call of nature, is likely to get you out of your sleeping bag while the wild chorus continues.

Wolves may be dangerous to men. Sick ones, stricken with rabies, obviously are. But in their natural state they mostly seem moved by curiosity about humans, just as we are curious about them.

I recall one day when I dropped our exploration leader Bill Brisbin and another geologist, in two adjacent areas.

They went armed only with rock hammers and specimen bags because they only expected to be on the site for a couple of hours.

As it turned out I picked up the other man first. He had worked hard and grunted as he loaded his rock trophies in the chopper. A few minutes later we dropped down to recover Brisbin, who appeared before us running, dishevelled and somewhat distraught. His face and arms were scratched and he clutched an empty rock bag in one hand and clenched his rock hammer in the other.

"Wolves," he said, laconically. When he calmed down we found out that the plural was an exaggeration. It was a single wolf, a big one, with no fear of humans and plenty of ability to put the wind up prospectors.

Brisbin, soon after I had left him, had started to work the side of an outcropping. As he started whacking away at the rock seams he had an uncomfortable feeling he was being wathced. He glanced up and jumped a couple of feet when he noticed a large wolf looking down at him from a spot near the top of the slope. The wolf showed no fear of Brisbin but appeared intrigued by the tapping of his hammer. He even moved a step or two closer, as if he was trying to see just what was going on. Brisbin thought about the visitation. He stepped forward a couple of steps. The wolf backed up just the same distance. Bill moved back several paces. The wolf advanced. The ritual dance went on for several minutes, each passing second increasing the tension that was spreading through Brisbin's nervous system. He began to wonder if he was to be the man to prove that Jim Curran was the fibber. Slowly Brisbin backed up toward an evergreen tree some distance behind him. It was as casual a retreat as he could make it. The wolf advanced, never closing the gap but always at the same pace and distance. Occasionally it growled and bared a set of fangs that would have delighted Jack London. They roused no such feelings in Brisbin who eventually found he had backed himself up against the evergreen. With a leap he sprang into its branches, shinnying up to what he considered a safe distance above ground.

And there he clung. He swears the wolf grinned as he looked at the scientist spread-eagled in the pine needles. The furry monster obviously enjoyed the stalemate for he sat down at the foot of the tree and refused to budge.

This condition prevailed for a couple of hours until the wolf heard my helicopter approaching. Wolves hate choppers. All wild animals do. The noise does something to them. In this case it lifted the siege of Brisbin. With a final growl the wolf trotted off into the bush and Brisbin, still shaken by the experience, accumulated a few more scrapes as he slid down to earth and ran for the helicopter.

In my experience bears are much more of a nuisance, and much more dangerous to humans, than wolves. They are so big they can injure without intending to harm. And if they get angry, look out. They can inflict lethal damage with their claws, arms and teeth.

Black bears seldom bother people. We found them timid and as long as we did not tolerate their presence, and regularly burned or disposed of our garbage, which is what tempts them, they posed no real danger. But if you let them stick around your camp they'll become a nuisance. Each visit increases their boldness and a bear on the hunt for food, or seized with curiosity, or angered, can completely wreck a camp.

One big black monster was giving us trouble in the Yukon

and we were in a quandary trying to figure out how to get rid of him. The problem was still unsolved when two Indians walked into camp and asked if we had seen any bear in the region. We welcomed them and told them to go no farther. They remained as our overnight guests, staking themselves out within range of the garbage dump. A couple of timely shots from their rifles disposed of our problem.

Grizzlies, of course, are another dish of bush tea. They never take no for an answer. They're mean, unpredictable and highly dangerous. And they have the instincts of a human in their hunting habits, with highly-developed stalking skills that are truly frightening.

On a number of occasions while airborne, I spotted grizzlies apparently tracking men on the ground. Their stalking seemed deliberate. They remained at a distance, apparently following the men through their keen sense of smell. I was able to warn my associates and usually to drive off the bears with a few passes in my chopper.

In the Yukon, one day, I noted an enormous grizzly moving swiftly along the trail and only a couple of hundred yards from our camp, which he was rapidly approaching. I could see no one around and it was possible that this intruder would have wrecked the camp before anyone was able to interfere.

I dropped down, right over him, moving around so that he first stopped, then turned around and retraced his steps to a small river. There I hustled him to the far bank, then turned him around and chased him back through the water. After four or five such trips the bear took off at top speed. The last I saw of him he was disappearing into the bush with amazing rapidity, about as fast as his 700 or 800 pounds of muscle could move him. The speed with which these magnificent animals can move is truly amazing. I would hate to have to try to outrun one.

Few people who are careful need to engage in that sort of sprinting, although I can recall a new, young pilot who created some sort of panic when he flushed what he thought was a brown bear not far from camp. With some aerial flourishes he herded the panicked bear through the center of the camp, laughing heartily as he watched people diving in all directions to get out of the way. Fortunately, the bear was even more frightened and just kept going and eventually disappeared. The pilot landed, laughing hard at his little joke, and was almost lynched by an angry mob of compatriots who pointed out that the animal was no brown bear but a large, angry grizzly and that an immediate course in bear identification was required.

More aggravating, persistent and even dangerous to humans are much smaller forms of life. These are the swarms of flies and mosquitos, which come in numbers that have to be experienced to be believed.

Aside from the personal irritation they cause there is a definite danger in operating near them, for the whirling rotor blades of a helicopter become caked with insect bodies as they move through the thick swarms of these pests.

The resulting gooey mess can spoil the air flow over the blades, thus spoiling their effective lifting force. The effect is very much like 'icing' in the cold Arctic skies, and damn nearly as dangerous.

No rookie pilot can ever appreciate these natural perils of wilderness flying from lectures in training school. I have mentioned several of them. Among the problems is that of working across water on a dead calm day.

Unless there is a ripple on the water depth perception vanishes and it becomes difficult to tell the height of your machine above the water surface. The same technical problem arises on large, frozen lakes in winter time. On a large lake, glassy water is particularly hazardous in the waning light conditions of dusk. You really have no idea of your height above water. In a fixed-wing float plane, if you are coming in for a landing, you set up your flight path at a descent of about 200 feet per minute and maintain a careful watch on everything in your landing attitude. The trick is to shut off your power as soon as your floats touch the water.

In the case of a float-equipped helicopter the problem is met differently. You drop down slowly and as your machine gets close to the water the downdraft creates ripples that provide the third dimensional information. But even that isn't absolutely guaranteed. I found my skids in the water before I knew it one time just at dusk while crossing a mile-wide lake heading for a landing pad we had built over the water. This was an unusual place for it but there wasn't enough room on the camp site for the landing pad. In this case I was using skids and making a slow approach.

At the moment the skids went under, water deluged the helicopter, pouring over the plastic control section top in a cascade. Fortunately I reacted quickly and had time enough to pull straight up before being capsized.

Snow conditions on a flat surface give you the same trouble for if there are no rocks on the snow, or any trees nearby, there is no vision comparison. Even a man standing in the snow can provide the yardstick you need under these conditions.

Wilderness flying has produced its own remedies for the special problems associated with it. Much of the north, most of it in fact, is muskeg. Frequently, you have to land people in the muskeg, a dangerous pad on which to set down a chopper. Muskeg is muck in which higher tufts of grass abound, big enough to upset a machine unless its weight is evenly distributed among them. Skids are useless in these conditions. Helicopter men have conquered the problem by fashioning 'bear paw' attachments on the rear of the skids.

These are oblong sheets of aluminum, with one blunt end. The flat surface is perforated so that when the chopper is set down on the sticky muskeg it will be able to lift off with a minimum of suction resistance from the paw. These contrivances are about 18 in. wide and 30 in. long, and they act much like snowshoes in distributing weight. They are invaluable in the summer of the Northland.

Because of the special hazards of frontier flying, it would appear that constant and detailed supervision of planes and pilots ought to be the rule. In all my years of northern flying I never once was personally inspected by anyone from the Canadian Department of Transport, whose responsibility it is to look after these things. No one has ever checked load, the condition of the craft, or asked to make sure all checks have been done, or tried to really ascertain if the craft was serviceable.

The truth is that in the North particularly, although it

happens elsewhere, heavily overloaded craft are taking off all the time.

This is particularly true where float planes are operating on large lakes or rivers and where their takeoff runway can go on for miles. It is different on small bodies of water with their limited runways. I've seen chance-taking pilots run float planes up on the shore trying to get airborne.

I remember one occasion when the pilot twice ran ashore. We pushed him off each time and he finally got away on his third attempt. Planes are loaded until the backs of the floats are submerged, a sure sign of dangerous overloading, but away they go.

In the case of a chopper, an overloaded machine merely refuses to rise, and you lighten load to the point where it will. But even that can be dangerous for you may be beyond proper weight capacity and manage to get airborne by using full bore, a condition that means you have no spare power and no safety margin in case of an emergency. It's illegal, of course, and obviously wrong, but the hard truth is that a pilot in the North who refuses to take off with overloads and insists on sticking to legal limits will very quickly be replaced. It's as simple as that. Regardless of what is said about operators being so careful and insistent that everything be done according to the book, it just isn't so.

In remote areas, it will be argued, there is no way transport officials can keep their fingers on activities. The remedy really lies in the hands of the pilots and the associations that are supposed to represent them, and, of course, in the protests of the passengers whose well-being is hazarded by these dangerous practices.

There are many places in the North, such as Inuvik, where dozens of airplanes fly in and out every day. There is no reason why the Department can't step up safety measures by locating inspectors to make spot checks that cover some of the important things they prefer to ignore.

Innovation is left pretty much to the flyers themselves. In communications, for example, we tried supplying ground parties with hand-held flares by which they could signal their positions to us. These are smoke generators about two inches in diameter and five inches long. They are ignited by removing one end and striking the head like a safety match. Brilliant orange smoke of great density and quantity pours out, and for some time we used these flares to the satisfaction of all concerned. Our party chief was so delighted with them that he sent a message to Calgary ordering a gross of them. The response was immediate and not what he expected. The flares, headquarters pointed out, cost more than $4 each and they couldn't imagine what we proposed to do with a gross of them, and refused to fill the order.

I have no doubt that the people back at head office are puzzled many times a year at the many strange requests from field parties. It reminds me of a story they used to tell about the two prospectors who sent a message to their expediter in Edmonton. "Ship at once two punts and a canoe," they telegraphed. They were working in shallow water and muskeg and it was too deep and dangerous to wade and far too shallow for power boats. Communications in the north aren't all they might be at times, thanks to mountain ranges, magnetic deposits and plain old static, but these worthies still were astonished when the answer got back a couple of days later. "First two items en route," read the message, "but what in hell is a panoe?"

For a time the ground parties signalled their position with smoke from fires, not the safest or best method of letting us know where they were. This went on until I came up with the idea of supplying each man with a yard-square piece of fluorescent orange nylon cloth that could be vigorously waved as the chopper approached. I'm not claiming that I originated this simple, effective method of communication but I have been delighted to see that it is now in common use in northern flying.

Through the long daylight hours of the northern summer, sleep sometimes is difficult and time hangs heavy. Radio reception is uncertain, often too poor to be worth the listening. Television is something left behind in the last centers of civilization, although satellite communication may change that in the future. Working parties amuse themselves. They play cards, read and eat. It is a skimpy entertainment program and anything that will diversify it is welcomed.

From time to time we had visitors and occasionally they provided an extra challenge for some part of the camp establishment. There was the evening Jim Grady flew in with an apprentice engineer, a young man who kept telling us he had never landed on the top of a mountain, until Jim promised he would see that he did on their return trip.

Off they flew . . . and a short time later they were back at their own camp with a damaged chopper, all because that young fellow wanted to land on the top of a mountain.

Jim confessed he had been a bit nonchalant as he demonstrated the art of mountain-top landing and he had neglected to circle to find the right wind direction. Updrafts lift you and downdrafts pull you down and you need to know which is prevailing.

He started to descend, found himself in a downdraft and was sucked over the edge of the mountain top, hitting the slope several times. He poured on full bore and got away safely, but not before the undercarriage struck some rocks and the upright connecting the starboard skid to the ship was smashed.

The chopper hovered as the ground staff pondered how to get it down without more damage. Engineer Hans Nixdorf, one of the sharpest of his kind I ever ran across, set out a 10-gallon drum so that Jim could put the machine down on its crossbar with no weight on the skid.

Nixsdorf then went to work on the damage. He spent hours straightening the skid, then emptied a dozen 48-ounce fruit juice cans, removed the ends and split them down the side. He wrapped them around the broken 'leg', bound them tightly, drilled holes through them and bolted the whole thing together. It worked beautifully until new parts arrived.

In our moments of ease at one camp we devised an exercise that used up the many empty insecticide spray cans. These contain a goodly charge of energy even when empty and we found a way to tap it, with an improvised cannon fashioned from a length of abandoned pipe. We air-lifted the pipe out to Dawson City where we had it welded shut at one end. (It was rather an expensive deal but we overlooked this.) Placed in the fire the artillery piece would become red hot at which point a spray can inserted into it could be made to soar into the air with a loud bang, lifting a couple of hundred feet into the sky and far enough away from camp to disconcert roosting birds and scare the devil out of any stray grizzlies.

When we ran out of spray cans, which was inevitable, one enterprising member of the group discovered that a small tin of fruit or tomatoes was the right calibre for the field piece. They went off with an equally impressive roar, although they took somewhat longer to reach the explosion point, showering the countryside with fruit salad and vegetables. When entertainment and pastimes have to be home-made, you use what is available!

In camp the food usually is good and plentiful but the variety is limited. One summer we got pork so often that my stomach turned at the sight of a chop. I concluded that irritation on my next trip to Telegraph Creek by telling the supplier there, Steel Hyland, to order nothing but beef. When I returned to camp I informed a puzzled cook that there was a sudden, continent-wide shortage of pork and that it was unlikely we would get any more than year.

For long-standing reasons, some of them justified and some fancies, cooks have always been the subject of bad jokes and worse criticism wherever two or three or more diners are gathered. Some cooks were really good. Some tried hard. Some were terrible, but anyplace I have been there was a tendency to lump them all together under the last label. Cooks learn to live with it or die of ulcers. I recall one day when our cook slaved away from dawn to dinner time and stood back beaming at his culinary triumph, awaiting the verdict. He got it, from my engineer, who sat down, took one look at his plate and said, in a very loud voice, "This stuff would gag a maggot." No wonder some cooks take to drinking up the cooking sherry, and the vanilla extract.

# 7

# Go Fly, Young Man

Few jobs will provide a young man with as much opportunity to see the world and its rapidly shrinking frontiers than that of pilot in charter or leased helicopter services.

It certainly has broadened my knowledge of distant places, and the way in which science and technology are combining to make the crooked straight and the rough places plain.

After my opening stint in the Yukon when I had my first brush with disaster, I moved into a longish term of duty with the maintenance crews of Westcoast Transmission's gas pipeline from northern B.C. to the U.S. border.

Okanagan had signed a contract with Westcoast to service the line, fly safety checks along its lengthening range, and help plot the new cuts through the bush for pipe laying. It was a three-helicopter assignment on a seven-day work week. We were based at Fort St. John in the Peace River country and I was one of two pilots. The third helicopter was a spare, to provide insurance for daily maintenance of services if one machine should become unserviceable.

As it turned out the other pilot became ill after about 10 weeks on the job and had to be taken to Vancouver for treatment. A replacement was promised so I wasn't too worried when the chief pilot telephoned to ask if I could hang on alone for a couple of weeks until a second pilot could be sent. This was no great chore for a couple of weeks.

91

It was only when I found myself doing a single seven months later that I began to be somewhat annoyed.

It was clear the company had saved itself the price of a second pilot at my expense—and without so much as a thank you or an extra dollar in my pay cheque.

I put in about 900 flying hours on that particular job and survived the remoteness and hard work primarily, I guess, because it was a truly fascinating experience. My role was to move men and equipment around, an assignment giving me a close look at what was going on and how a pipeline is built and maintained in the heart of the bushlands.

Some of the men I flew were specialists in putting 'pigs' through the line. This had nothing to do with the hungry grunters whose fate is to decorate the dining room table in the form of bacon, ham and pork chops. 'Pigs,' in a pipeline, are devices that look like a set of the wheels used on railway cars, although they are not quite so large. They have rubber rings around the wheel rims for smoother going and to avoid wear on the interior of the pipe in which they work. They are an exact fit for the interior dimensions of the line through which they are forced by gas pressure, the rubber acting like a squeegee to push out moisture, liquid that may have accumulated, and any other obstructive matter. The liquid material is removed and processed, in this case at the Taylor Flats scrubbing plant south of Fort St. John, which accounts for the huge yellow mounds of sulfur that have accumulated there, sulfur being a major constituent of natural gas.

From time to time I took visitors along with me. One of my first passengers was Dan Murray from the Alaska Highway News, a son of the celebrated 'Ma' Murray, the delightfully outspoken eccentric who has run a weekly newspaper in the B.C. Interior at Lillooet and Bridge River for years, challenging politicians, preachers and the pompous with a clamor that sometimes reached international attention.

I flew Dan around to get some air pictures of the Fort St. John region, a service that so delighted him he sent me a free subscription to his newspaper, The **Alaska Highway News,** but not so much that he could refrain from cancelling it the day I moved out of the area.

When you're isolated like that, some 800 miles from the city of Vancouver, little things make a big impression and small hurts can rankle. That Christmas, I awaited with some anticipation the arrival of a bonus check or turkey that I had been told Okanagan handed out to employees at the holiday season.

It was a long wait, for I have received neither to this day. Some time after they became overdue I wrote to the company's secretary-treasurer notifying him that the Christmas remembrance had gone astray and that nothing had been received by my engineer, Lloyd McKenzie, or me.

He returned an astonishingly philosophical answer. Christmas, he noted, was past, and would have to be written off as a bit of bad luck, with the hope that my luck would turn the next time. It was a cavalier response that prompted me to put in an expense account for $18, enough to provide a bottle of spirits and some creature comforts for Lloyd and me, about the equivalent of the price of a couple of turkeys in those days. It was a mild fraud that no one challenged, but it was no more than our due, and made the two of us feel a whole lot better way up there in the wilderness.

A first-class engineer is a vital part of any chopper team and I was lucky to have McKenzie with me on this assignment. He inherited some miserable jobs with good humor, one of them in the dead of winter when my machine had engine trouble at Mile 73 on the Alaska Highway.

It was a point I used to visit frequently for it had a roadside cafe with good coffee. One day, when the thermometer was registering 35 deg. below zero, I set down for a warmup mug of the brew and noticed that my magnetos were malfunctioning. I telephoned to Fort St. John and notified Lloyd, who motored out to my rescue. It took some time, three days to be exact, before he could make the 'copter flyable. It was a rotten 72 hours for him, working under a makeshift canvas tent draped around the stalled machine. In the end he had to change the harness, which is the ignition system wiring, and replace all the plugs and the magnetos. Lloyd put a small heater in the tent but it was so cold he had to knock off work every 20 or 30 minutes and make a fast dash into the cafe to get warm. He repaired that machine on hot coffee and sheer determination and how he escaped frostbite I'll never know. It made me glad that I was a pilot and not an engineer.

Our helicopters were fitted with FM radio, small two-way receiver-transmitters about half the size of a shoe box and linked to a control room that Westcoast maintained at Fort St. John. All the Westcoast trucks were similarly equipped and the circuit was assisted by a booster tower on top of a hill at Mile 101 that increased the signal enough to provide good relays.

The tower was 192 feet high, with an antenna attached to it. One day the company decided they wanted to move the antenna and were about to call in a team of tower specialists when I suggested the job could be done easier, quicker and cheaper by using a helicopter. I knew the site, for I flew by it every day.

They were doubtful but company officials agreed to give it a try, a decision that obliged their radio man on the site to climb, gingerly, up to the top of the tower. There, while I hovered above the tower, he undid the four bolts that held the antenna in place. When he was ready I lowered a chain and hook and he made sure it was attached to the antenna. Within seconds it was safely whisked away. I don't know whether the radio man got danger pay. He should have, for the firm saved a lot of money. Those tower specialists draw down big pay.

Westcoast had begun cutting a new line through the bush from Mile 101 on a course charted by ground surveyors. I persuaded them that the helicopter could help by taking them aloft to see the terrain over which they had to work. I did better than that, too, for I would hover in the sky giving them a sight for their transits.

The actual route was cut through by bulldozer men, genuine artists whose skill at levelling rough country in a direct line still amazes me. In time, I was made responsible for flying supplies and fuel to the bulldozer men, saving them a good deal of time previously wasted in their laborious returns to get fresh supplies. All I did was put the supplies at the farthest point of advance each day, permitting the dozer

Flora Dora Hotel, Dawson City, 1958. First trip to Syd Lake. This is where we stayed.    *C. Weir*

Beginnings of forest fire. Mackenzie River area, North West Territories.    *C. Weir*

Work boat on Stikine River, B.C., moving from Wrangle to Telegraph Creek.

operator to stay in the bush for a week at a time. I don't think the operator was too thrilled with such efficiency—he missed his nightly beer at Mile 101.

Soon we were using the chopper for slow aerial searches on the unbroken country ahead, spotting boggy patches that ought to be avoided. Frequently I marked the best line of advance by dropping streamers fashioned from rolls of toilet paper that landed on the tree tops, a remarkably efficient and (at that time at least) inexpensive way to indicate direction. At the present price of toilet paper they ought to be using something with a salvage possibility.

It was a grand, wild country, abounding with moose and bear. The former, in season, meant fresh meat. Many of the line workers got moose tags and shot their limit. This was easy hunting, for most of the men ran into moose while they were working. The animals had a tendency to follow the newly cut right-of-way, because it was easier than walking through the bush.

Sometimes I gave the hunters an assist by dropping messages to them when I had spotted a moose. I guess this wasn't exactly kosher and I expect it is illegal today, but it seemed no sin then, there being so many moose about. I counted more than 70 in one day while flying a slow direct-line 70-mile leg out from Fort St. John. Moose steaks, properly prepared, are something an epicure can appreciate. I'm no gourmet but I liked them so much I got my own moose tag, but never found time to take one.

It was on this assignment that I had my first insight into the potential danger of static electricity, and once again it was the engineer who was the victim.

One winter's day, as I put the chopper down, I felt it was out of balance and vibrating. I called Lloyd over, lifted up a few feet and hollered to him to look and listen. Lloyd shook his head, apparently agreeing that something was wrong, and put one hand on the machine to check the vibration.

He jumped about six feet and almost landed on his back. "Shut her off," he shouted, "there's a bad short somewhere."

Lloyd looked and looked. He tested here and there but he couldn't locate any short-circuit. Finally we figured it out. It was very cold and dry and, in the low temperature, that hovering machine had built up a charge of electricity strong enough to kill a man with a weak heart.

My engineer made sure that never happened again. To the undercarriage, he fastened a metal ground cable that would trail on the ground before landing and provide a ground for any static buildup. It worked the same way those metal strips do that are fixed under automobiles for the same purpose.

Engineers could take a lot of verbal static from pilots but there was no reason to endanger them with the real kind!

A pilot quickly learns to respect the weather along the frontier where it can turn treacherous in a matter of minutes. In cases of doubt we elect to wait it out. Amateur pilots are not always as fearful, which may account for some of the unfortunate things that happen to them.

We were working the area around Mile 397 on the highway just northwest of The Summit one day. The weather was foul and we were waiting it out in a lodge. It was hard to believe that anyone could be flying in the rain and fog so it took us a couple of minutes to realize that we could hear the noise of a light plane somewhere up in all that mess. We rushed out and caught a glimpse of it. It was heading for the top of the pass, no easy place to get through in good conditions. There was nothing we could do so we sat back and waited for word of the inevitable tragedy.

A few minutes later we heard the plane engine again. It staggered into sight, just skimming the tree tops, and finally plopped down on the highway in front of the lodge. The pilot, a 60-year-old U.S. businessman, and his wife, white-faced with fright, slowly climbed out. The woman looked like death warmed over. She said that the stalling signal device on the wing, which activates a horn in the cabin when the aircraft approaches stalling speed, had been sounding from the time her husband suddenly realized his perilous position and had skimmed the machine around the menacing edges of the mountain walls that hemmed him in.

I can't imagine what he was doing up there. He must have been a rank amateur, to hazard two lives. He was unobservant, to boot, for he hadn't noticed an emergency landing strip along the side of the highway a few miles to the west. It

96

Author with Bell 47-G2 helicopter at (B.C.) near Yukon border.    C. W

Bell 47-G2 helicopter at Syd Lake.

Okanagan Helicopters' first whirlybird. 47-B3. Agricultural Model. Interior of B.C.    *Alf Stringer*

47-G1 helicopter landing. Geology survey mission looking for zinc. 1964.    *C. Weir*

Harbour View Hotel. Flowers Cove, Newfoundland. Camped next door in tent.    *C. Weir*

Norwegian boat "Melshorn" during seal hunt, March, 1976.
*Dr. Moore, Greenpeace Foundation*

Harp seal carcasses. Ice floes near Bell Isle, March, 1976.
"Norwegian kill."     *Patrick Moore, Greenpeace Foundation*

Helicopter crash on ice off Labrador Coast during seal hunt. Not author's machine. 1964.

Norwegian sealer with harp seal pelts. March, 1976. *Patrick Moore, Greenpeace Foundation*

Somewhere in Northern B.C.

Crash at Haines Junction, Yukon. Note tail section sticking out from front of machine. Main rotor blades iced-up, causing crash. 1960.    *C. Weir*

Bell 47-G3-B2 beside glacier in Northern B.C.    *Alf Stringer*

Refuelling on bush airstrip, N.W.T. Author on left. *C. Weir*

Bell 47-G3-B2. Geological survey for oil. *C. Weir*

Returning to camp after survey expedition.     *Alf Stringer*

Mile 427, Alaska Highway. Slinging an engine under the chopper for 35 mile flight. Exploratory drilling mission. *C. Weir*

Exploratory drill site. Northern B.C.

Topographical survey. Cairn in Northern B.C.

Rainbow Lake. Base camp for topographical survey for B.C. Government.    *C. Weir*

Bell 47-G3-B2. Topographical survey south of Watson Lake. *C. Weir*

Bell 204, 10 passenger helicopter.     *B.C. Forest Service*

U.S. Navy ice-breaker. Note helicopter pad on stern of ship. Greenland.

Sondersom S.A.C. Base.

Sondersom Strategic Air Command Base.

Dye 1 Radar site, Dew Line, 5,500 feet above sea level. Forty-five residents supplied by chopper.

Author's wife. Arrival in New Guinea. *C. Weir*

Lord Mountbatten opening new air strip. Mt. Hagen, New Guinea. Approximately 70,000 natives present. *C. Weir*

Mount Hagen and district natives in full regalia for visit of Lord Mountbatten. 1965. *C. Weir*

New Guinea natives gathered in front of thatched roof home.

Helicopter landing in native village. New Guinea. 1965.

New Zealand crash. Author couldn't release dump gates.

Glacier feeding into Stikine River, B.C.     *C. Weir*

Bell 47-G2 in Northern B.C.    *C. Weir*

Home in Inuvik.    *C. Weir*

S-55 Sikorsky. Author flew this helicopter on last mission in the Arctic. 1972. He is here inspecting machine in Vancouver before departure to Richardson Island of the Arctic Circle.     *C. Weir*

Winter camp. The sides of these mobile homes fold in to form a single unit with truck body. Richard Island, N.W.T.     *C. Weir*

Turbine S55 Sikorsky hauling 3,500 lbs. dynamite. N.W.T.

makes you wonder how some people manage to qualify as pilots. And it is proof that possession of a pilot's license doesn't necessarily mean that anyone is fit to fly a plane. The missing element is judgment, a quality that no exams can demonstrate and one that may only be discovered to be missing when it is too late to do anything about it.

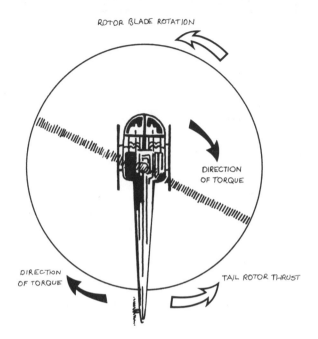

# 8

# Mid Canada Line

Periodically throughout my flying career I have been directly associated with the Royal Canadian Air Force, the now-departed service that helped me grow my pilot's wings. As I have recounted I found the R.C.A.F. unbearable in peace time, at least as a serving airman, but as a civilian, free from the strictures and inhibitions that envelop the man in uniform, I have found my association with it to be lively, useful, even enjoyable.

My path crossed that of the R.C.A.F. once more in 1959 when my assignment with Okanagan Helicopters, and later with another employer, Autair of Montreal, directed me to assist in servicing the Mid Canada Line, one of the three continent-wide radar defence systems set up by North American Air Defence Command (NORAD) to protect Canada and the U.S. against sneak air attacks over the North Pole.

There never was any doubt that it was a defence against air aggression from the Soviet Union, for no other power was in a position to strike this continent from that direction and the danger of attack from the south was considered so unlikely that no similar defence measures were ever erected there. The memory of those Singapore guns that could only fire out to sea was a chiller for anyone who thought seriously about the arrangements.

123

During the Cold War years, before Sputnik and intercontinental ballistic missiles, the system appeared justified. Hindsight suggests it was a waste of money, but defence planners cannot be blessed by hindsight, or aided by it in making vital judgments for defence today and tomorrow. What all of us can be happy about is that the system was never called upon to prove its worth, and that it had now been deactivated as unnecessary. It was the middle fence in a triple-tiered system that set down distant early warning (DEW) kube stations across the Far North, and the rather nebulous and never-completed Pinetree Line across the waist of the continent, roughly along the 49th Parallel. Mid Canada defence ran from Dawson Creek, B.C., on the west, to Goose Bay, Labrador, on the east—an expensive chain of installations with unmanned, automatic listening posts every 30 miles, and larger manned and more sophisticated regional stations every 300 miles. It cost millions to install and maintain.

For some years maintenance had been provided by the helicopters and pilots of Okanagan from Dawson Creek to Winisk, but in 1962 the B.C. firm was sharply under-bidden by Autair, which was awarded the servicing contract for three years in what turned out to be a classic example of why contracts should not always be awarded to the lowest bidder.

In preparation for my initial assignment, I took an Okanagan conversion course in Vancouver to fit me to handle Sikorsky S-55 choppers, six-passenger machines, larger and more intricate than the Bells I knew so well. After I had logged about nine hours on Sikorskys I was given a week's leave before proceeding by commercial plane to Winisk, Manitoba, one of the Mid Canada regional stations, situated about 600 miles northeast of Winnipeg. Like similar stations it had upwards of 125 men on the site, only two of them chopper pilots. There were three Okanagan helicopters on the base.

Our job was to service the unmanned stations for 150 miles in either direction of Winisk by ferrying technicians and fuel and replacement parts to them on a regular schedule. Each robot station was powered by three Diesel engines, of which two were always operational, and the data they ceaselessly collected was fed back to a central control computer for assessment.

The station commander, R.C.A.F. Squadron Leader Roy Greenaway, was a highly competent, affable chief whom I quickly learned to respect and appreciate. His was no easy job, for he had to keep men happy in a remote area where they were required to serve for months at a time. Until furlough, all ranks, and the civilians, had to find a way to get along in restricted conditions that inevitably produce tensions that turn abrasive in some people.

Greenaway, on the whole, succeeded admirably by a judicious mixture of firmness and good humor. Physically, the station was comfortable with the usual mess halls, dining rooms, a hospital, and other areas. But there was nowhere in that isolated area for anyone to go, except a Cree Indian village about six miles away, which itself had little to offer but a Hudson's Bay Company post, and whatever companionship could be found among the Indians, the factor and the village priest. Even that sort of communication was discouraged for, prior to my arrival, the village had been placed off limits except for those with special visiting authorization.

Even this infrequent touching of hands was strictly controlled, for Greenaway had pointed out the penalties of $500 fine and six months in jail for providing the Indians with liquor, and he had written his own rules to make sure none of the staff interfered with the Cree women.

Movies, games and other entertainment were regularly provided at the station but in general the sociability leaned heavily to horseplay, as it usually does in an all-male environment. Greenaway was wise enough to be tolerant and took in good part some of the juvenile pranks in which he found himself involved.

On one occasion the assistant cook, well awash in lager, passed out and was put to bed in Greenaway's room. The C.O. said nothing. He roused the inebriate and piloted him down the hall to the bed of one of the revelers, and tucked him in there.

During one rather riotous party, the C.O. found that his room had been stripped of all its furniture. Without turning

125

a hair he walked into the first empty cubicle, tucked himself in and slept peacefully through to breakfast time.

Greenaway wasn't above a small jest himself. Returning from a weekend at his Ottawa home, he secreted in his luggage a carton of issue condoms drawn from a mystified storeman in the nation's capital.

The sanitary system at Winisk was sewered into a large holding and treatment tank. The entire sanitary system was the special domain of a strict, humorless Irish engineer who ran it well and ruled with puritanical fervor.

A few days later this worthy came to Greenaway in a great state of agitation. "There are women on the base," he confided. "How can there be?" Greenaway demanded. "I don't know, sorr, but there are," the engineer insisted. "Come with me, I'll prove it," he added. He led the post commander to the treatment tank and with a dark scowl and jabbing forefinger pointed out a number of condoms floating around.

Greenaway conceded his amazement but insisted the engineer was in error. The sanitary officer sought vigilantly for the offenders but Greenaway never told this frustrated hunter that he had been flushing a condom or two into the system for several days to start this March hare.

Greenaway fought hard to overcome boredom, including his own. One way was to learn to fly a helicopter. He was a qualified fixed-wing pilot but knew nothing about choppers, although I found him an excellent pupil.

He had his most difficult task in protecting the Indian women from the white men for enforcing his non-fraternization rule was almost impossible, thanks to the reluctance of some of the protected to shelter under it. One day it was reported that two enterprising young Cree females had quietly constructed a small shack near the station dump from boards, sheeting and other discarded materials, and were busy offering female compansionship, at a price, to a steady procession of visitors from the station.

Greenaway ordered the shack burned to the ground. For a few days all was in order. Then the word came that a new shack was open for business. So the war went with the results inconclusive, and it may well be that some of the underlings assigned to the destruction of this ramshackle house of joy had some secret sympathies with the young women who were demonstrating how well they had been imbued with the virtues of private enterprise.

I visited the Indian village at least once a week, as I had the task of flying the Roman Catholic padre to the post to conduct religious services for the sheep of his flock. It wasn't the only time I was assigned the duty of picking up the padre. It happened at several northern stations but it always struck me as odd that only the R.C. clergy were hauled in, and left me wondering if the Protestants had no need of clerical attention or had been written off as irreversible sinners.

As a result, I got to know the village, clustered around the HBC post, and its inhabitants quite well. The priest, a gentle French Canadian, ran the village school and quite clearly was devoted to his dark-eyed charges and the fulfillment of his duties in this otherwise God-forsaken spot.

Taking coffee with him in his small home one day I was shocked to learn that he was paying exorbitant prices at the trading post for essentials such as coffee, tea and gasoline. I had long felt that the HBC monopoly, so evident across the north, meant ripoff prices for the natives but somehow I had expected to find that the priestly schoolmaster and shepherd of the flock would not be among those fleeced.

Back at the station we had masses of everything, for the indent system functioned regardless of usage. At one time we had enough floor wax on hand to last 15 years. There was so much that someone got annoyed and sent back five tons of it in a C-111 Flying Boxcar freighter to make room in the storehouse for something more useful. There were stacks of cases, full of 48-ounce jars of coffee, and dozens more cases of artificial cream, enough to last for a couple of generations. I thought of the poor padre paying 70 cents for 2½ ounces of coffee. The next time I visited him my engineer and I walked in, each carrying a carton, one of coffee and one of cream.

"What on earth is that?" said the good Father. "Just a little coffee," I told him. He looked pleased but puzzled.

"It wouldn't be stolen?" he felt constrained to ask.

I never flinched as I answered, "Of course not, Father,

you know me better than that." In a way it wasn't even a white lie. In the service the only real crime is to steal the mess whisky: tea and coffee don't count.

Around Christmas of that year my relationship with the Indians jumped up several notches. Hunting had been poor and the prospect of fresh moose meat for the Christmas dinner looked remote. The Indian men tramped miles on their snowshoes and came back empty-handed and more discouraged every day as Christmas approached.

Then, one day, someone passed a small miracle. As I flew along from the village to the station I spotted three moose rolling along through the drifts. They looked fat and healthy, ready for the roasting pan. At the station I informed Greenaway, who sent word to the Cree chief who happened to be one of the civilian workers at the camp. With the C.O.'s blessing the chief and I took off for the village, where he donned hunting garments and where we were joined by the chief's brothers, both of whom came well-armed with rifles and snowshoes at the ready.

My plan had been to put them down near the moose, then return when the hunt was over. They had more sensible ideas, arguing that they could hunt from the chopper much more easily than by ploughing through the snow. I moved in slowly on the moose; and my passengers, lying on their bellies on the floor of the cabin, picked off the Yuletide meat without wasting a shot. Then I flew back to camp where they assembled some sleighs and a few extra hands and went out to retrieve the game.

I was genuinely touched, and mightily surprised, a few weeks later when I was formally presented with a pair of beaded moosehide gauntlets made from the skins of the animals, a gesture of thanks for my help in providing the Crees with a Merry Christmas.

It wasn't quite the last I heard of that airborne hunt. The ease with which we had knocked over the moose delighted almost everyone in the tribe. The exception was the village sourpuss, a man I was told later who was a constant troublemaker. It appears that he had spotted the moose and had kept the news to himself, hoping to bag them as they came closer to the camp, to earn the prestige, and the rewards, for himself. He pretended to be outraged by this hunting from the helicopter and demanded that the village priest write to the authorities and report this breach of the game laws. Fortunately for all of us, he couldn't read or write and somehow the priest never found time to pen the letter—a good thing, for I might have lost my licence had the complainant been able to press his case.

Christmas at the station followed service tradition with a few local flourishes. At Winisk, for example, the officers and senior civilian staffers, opened the yule proceedings by preparing a huge urn of breakfast punch. It was placed on a trolley, along with a battery-operated record player, and trundled through the living quarters where the sleepers were aroused with Christmas carols and steaming mugs of paint-remover-strength brew stout enough to floor a bull moose. It is a tribute to the sturdiness of Canada's airmen that not a man missed Christmas dinner, at which, as is the custom, the officers acted as the mess hall waiters while the men dined.

We had an organized program and it barely stopped until all were ready to retire, or be carried to bed. It was a necessary precaution, for Christmas in the outposts of the nation can be a melancholy occasion unless things are planned to fill the day.

Operations out of Winisk were normal for the most part. My closest brush with danger came when I moved three engineers to one of the unmanned sites and, unknown to me, the helicopter engine oil breather froze over and the oil was forced out of the filler cap and sprayed all over the rear portion of the cabin. Looking ahead I did not see it and none of my passengers mentioned the odd coating of oil accumulating around and above them. As I put the machine down I was horrified to discover I had lost almost all my oil and was within a couple of minutes of a seize-up that would have meant a crash-landing in the snowy wilderness.

I radioed to Winisk and we hunkered down and waited until a fresh supply of oil could be flown out in one of the other choppers.

Winisk had a sergeants' mess, although there was only one sergeant on the base, and he presided over a lively membership of civilian associates. As NCO messes do the world over, I swear they made much more fun than the officers, and some carousing and partying that would have been hard to equal.

One night that winter they had a good one going, 60 or more on hand, none feeling any pain. One of the group, who stepped outside to relieve himself, rushed back in unbuttoned and shouting there was a polar bear outside. "Oh yeah," his companions jeered. "Get lost," they added. But he insisted until someone peeked out and screamed, "Migawd, there really is a bear out there." Whereupon the room emptied, the celebrants fighting one another to be first outside. Sure enough, there was a bear, a great big one, eight or nine feet tall, shadowy white about 30 feet away and striding slowly towards the camp light. The bear blinked, growled and took another step, at which everyone outside tried to get back into the mess at once. They fought their way in and bolted the door. The bear backed away. The curious came out. The bear moved forward and they bolted back inside. So it went until the bear tired of the game, turned and started loping down the road towards the camp fire hall.

Someone had enough sense to telephone the duty firemen that a bear was heading their way. Polar bears make lovely pictures, they can be turned into beautiful rugs, they delight children visiting the zoo, but they're damn dangerous around a camp, particularly when they're hungry.

The firemen, who had no desire to risk wrestling a bear on a fire call, dispatched the bear with a couple of blasts from a shotgun.

We didn't see many bears at Winisk but there are hundreds of them in a colony that congregates near Fort Churchill every year, and scare the wits out of the inhabitants of that Hudson Bay port.

Winisk's sole link to the outside was by air, making it vitally important to maintain the single runway on the base, on which RCAF and commercial planes landed and took off. Trans-Air DC4s, on a Monday flight from Winnipeg to Montreal via Churchill and Winisk, and return Tuesday, used it once a week, and the RCAF was in and out all the time.

The air link to the rest of the world was useful in setting up

130

one of the best, or worst, jokes I can remember. It was only possible because the deputy station commander at Winisk was very steamed up about a young lady in Great Whale.

One Friday afternoon an RCAF plane with a six-man crew came in for an overnight stay, en route to Churchill. I called them aside and said: "We've got a chap working here who has a girl friend at Great Whale. You'll meet him in the bar this evening but don't tell him or anyone you're bound for Churchill. If they ask, say you're going to Great Whale and I guarantee this fellow will want a ride up there for the weekend." They agreed to play. Great Whale was about 300 miles east of Winisk and Churchill farther than that in the other direction.

Sure enough, they were asked by the prospective victim where they were heading, and they told him, "to Great Whale." He was delighted. "Say, would you have room for just one passenger?" he asked. "Sure," they told him, "Just be down at the hangar about 0:700."

Sharp at seven the hitch-hiker appeared, shining with spit and polish, clean shirt, suitcase and a gift parcel. His friends invited him aboard, made sure he was comfortable, and unloaded him at Churchill several hours later, assuring him he had been mistaken and that they had told him they were going to Churchill, and not to Great Whale, and blamed the 'misunderstanding' on the alcoholic fog that crept into the mess hall.

Runway snow clearance was the task for a man who operated a high-powered snowblower, a mighty instrument he was expected to put into action in any kind of weather. One day he started out in a 'white-out' condition of visibility, bravely beating a path along the streets to the runway. With vision down to zero he went more by guess than by anything else, something that accounted for his removing first a fire hydrant, and then all the lower floor windows in a long office building. The pressure of the blown snow smashed in the lot and filled the offices with white stuff. It was no surprise when he was quietly and quickly removed from his snow blower assignment and banished from the outraged reach of all those trying to retrieve service bumph in the melting piles of snow.

After several months I was granted a week's leave, after which I was reassigned to Stoney Mountain, another Mid Canada station about 250 miles northeast of Edmonton. This post had to be reached via a DC-3 service to Fort McMurray, which wasn't much of a place a dozen years ago. McMurray is a much bigger, busier place today, thanks to gas fields and oil sands development, but at that time the main street was the main landing pad for helicopters.

My flight had been delayed and when I arrived I found that the helicopter I was to use had been waiting for me in McMurray and that the crew which flew it out was going on leave and would not be returning with it. The Mid Canada station, which I had never seen, was 25 miles away. I didn't know the country, it was getting dark and I viewed the whole journey with misgiving.

Common sense said, "Wait until morning," but the departing crew scoffed at my fears, gave me directions to the station and insisted on seeing me take off. It was only then I discovered I was in a machine with no landing lights, heading for a landing pad that, I discovered too late, lacked both landing lights and directional signals.

By good luck I spotted the station before realizing I would have to get down on my own. I circled it several times, then set the machine down by the light of a single bulb on a pole at the end of the hangar. I guess they thought I was a bit touched.

Weekends at Stoney Mountain offered a break, for I had to fly to McMurray every Saturday afternoon and return Sunday morning with the padre, flying him back to McMurray on Sunday afternoon and returning that night. I always had a full load of passengers with lots of volunteers offering to go along for a night on the town. It was an arrangement open to abuse, and abused it was. The visitors to McMurray celebrated in the usual way. I didn't mind their Saturday night sprees but I wasn't amused when they arrived for the return trip on Sunday still partying and in no shape to go anywhere but to bed.

Their hangovers were their own business, but flying the chopper was very much mine. Sometimes my passengers couldn't stagger across the street to the machine and had to be helped to the takeoff point and lifted into the cabin. In the passenger compartment the pilot's feet are exposed, and drunks can, and did, reach out and grab them, a most dangerous business for a pilot needs to have them free at all times to run his ship properly.

to *
p 135

As for Greenland, that clergyman who wrote the hymn about Greenland's icy mountains and India's coral strands ought to have been working on the DEW line to get the real feel of it. I'm certain he would have wondered, as so many have, why that big hunk of ice-capped real estate is called Greenland. It is the twin brother of Labrador, with glaciers, lands that God would have given to Cain except that I'm sure he would have refused to take the deeds to them.

move
to
*
p 145

Sondrestrom, just the same, is a lot better than most of the country around it, which isn't saying much. The base is situated on a plateau at the end of a long fiord in a setting as bare as an Irish pub after a bomb warning. It is an uninviting mixture of rocks and coarse sand on which the Americans, with beaver-like tenacity, have built an airstrip to service the SAC B-52 bombers, and a small town in which the servicing personnel can live, 2000 of them, bored to tears as they eke out service terms of up to 18 months.

Sondrestrom's excuse for existing is to maintain a fleet of air tankers capable of refueling B-52 fuel tanks in mid-air. These C-135 Globemasters are at the ready 24 hours a day, come rain or shine, and there was precious little of the latter and more snow than rain. Because it was there, Sondrestrom was given a minor role as a stopover location for Scandinavian Air Services flights to Los Angeles. Nothing grows there except the human hope of leaving this eternal desolation.

It's a humbling thought, just the same, to suspect that two or three thousand years hence some eager-beaver college kids on a vacation dig may be excavating the site and excitedly exclaiming about the artifacts left behind that crumbled outpost of that short-lived American empire of the 20th Century.

They will undoubtedly wonder about these big Globemasters that held some 10,000 gallons of a propellant called jet fuel which they flew up into the sky to transfer to

133

other big planes loaded with primitive nuclear bombs that were more than adequate for the task of destroying the world of that time.

In Sondrestrom I had my periods of such day-dreaming but most of the time I was busy looking after the 45 inhabitants of Dye-One, a base that could only be approached by air and around which there was no closed season on high velocity winds.

Sondrestrom and its environs, as the atlas makers call centres of human habitation, was an eye-opener for me. I had been hurried to the station from Toronto via Dover Air Force Base, N.J., where I had been loaded into one of those giant U.S. Air Force transport planes filled with some more people and a vast quantity of general cargo destined for Sondrestrom.

They seemed to have everything on board. I wandered around during the flight and discovered that, among other things, there were 10,000 dozen well-packed eggs on board and a proportionate amount of ham and bacon. Obviously the breakfasts were going to be first rate.

My assignment was to pilot a six-passenger Sikorsky helicopter, a fine machine with good range and carrying capacity. Most days I would haul supplies to Dye-One, just about everything you could imagine such a post might need, except liquor and females.

There is a puritanical insistence that women are unnessary and highly undesirable additions to such bases. Servicemen, it seems, are supposed to swear off sex in remote bases. In two world wars Americans were barred from legal brothels. The practical British, in North Africa at least, used their military police to maintain order in the queues that formed outside these establishments. In mixed headquarters the occasional American beat his country's MPs by borrowing a British chum's uniform. Sondestrom is no combined headquarters and the U.S. preference for an all-male environment persisted, at least as long as I was there, although women's lib may have changed things a bit, even in the ranks of the uniform wearers.

There were some girls at Sondrestrom but their presence only added to the feeling of deprivation because they were

134

Danish employees in the airline transit hotel, and 'off limits' as far as the Americans were concerned.

The DEW line sites were manned by civilians and their remoteness was such that it was probably a good thing that women and booze were not allowed on the premises. The liquor prohibition, in particular, made sense, although I knew of a few sharp cookies who found ways of getting a small stock of liquor into the site from time to time. Officially, at least, the only concession to King Alcohol was a ration of six cans of beer per week, hardly enough to spark bacchanalian revels.

The law against hard liquor put the best brains on the station to figuring out ways to break it without getting caught. I guess, like other chopper pilots, I winked at some of the infractions that served the spirituous ends of the outposted crews. I am sure that a lot of those cases labelled, "Fragile, flat gain amplifiers" gurgled when I lifted them.

Pilots, under special instruction not to fly liquor, were inclined to turn the blind eye to the facts if the labelling came within legitimate terms of reference. They knew those amplifiers were 40-oz. bottles of whisky but they weren't about to make a federal case of it.

The situation came to a head when one of the carousers grabbed my leg as we flew along several thousand feet up in the air. I told the station commander that in future I would not carry drunken passengers. He agreed with my decision and posted an order to that effect. Only a week later I left one drunk in Fort McMurray. He lost a week's pay but was totally sober when he reported for a flight back to base the following Sunday. His experience got the word around and the free loaders quickly realized that future flights involved a sense of passenger responsibility that would be enforced.

It wasn't all routine at Stoney. I was awakened one morning at three o'clock and told to fly to a manned outpost about 60 miles away and pick up a worker in need of emergency hospital treatment.

This particular facility was built on muskeg and had been constructed on pilings like a native hut on the banks of an African lake. The under part of the building was to have been closed off, but somehow the job wasn't completed and

135

a sudden cold spell had frozen all the water pipes and plumbing to iceberg condition. One of the station staff, waking in the middle of the night by a compulsion to relieve himself, recalled that there was no use using the bathroom. Half awake, he was able to reason that the closest and quickest place was the window. So he raised the metal frame and was blissfully getting rid of a load of beer when the window slipped and dropped like a guillotine, almost severing the extended member. Naturally he bled profusely, and his agony was indescribable. The emergency call by radio had alerted me but I had to wait for first light until I could take off and it was several hours more before I could lift the unfortunate man to McMurray where his sufferings were eased and he was flown to hospital in Edmonton. This has to be one of the most unusual and painful ways of being injured I have ever encountered. Fortunately, they didn't have to stitch on the whole thing, or he might have come up a bit short.

Some of the civvies at these outposts were the last of the gold rush breed. I think of a bull cook at Stoney, an aging citizen of the frontier who worked like a dog and finally saved up $5000 to fulfill a lifelong ambition to journey around the world. He got quite a sendoff before I flew him to McMurray on the weekend to wait for the commercial plane that would start him around the globe. I said goodbye and wished him *bon voyage* and had a farewell drink with him in the hotel bar.

A week later I returned—and he was still there, bleary-eyed and broke, with one of the meanest hangovers that ever afflicted mortal man. He had blown the bundle in a week and had nowhere to go but back to the kitchen. His around-the-world trip was a 28-mile flight to McMurray and back again.

It must have been someone like him who invented the hot seat installed in the mess for unwary visitors. It was a chair rigged with a Ford sparking coil on the underside, dead center. Nothing happened if the occupant merely sat down. But when he leaned back he activated an electrical connection that sent a strong enough jolt up the spine to put the ordinary victim into orbit. People who knew it was rigged sat around waiting for a new victim to appear. Some of these innocents sat straight down, and periodically they were forced back against the chair by willing hands anxious to provide another 'laugh'. It was pretty dim-witted stuff and it all ended very suddenly and for good when one victim suffered severe burns, and the hot seat was dismantled.

That spring I was taken off Mid Canada and did not return until March, 1962, when Autair was holding the contract. My first posting with Autair was back to Manitoba, at a station called Byrd, one much like the rest, distinguished only by my sharing a room with an associate who was a dangerous pyromaniac, as I quickly discovered. He liked to drink, and when intoxicated retired mumbling to bed where he broke all the station rules by lighting up cigarettes. On three occasions he set the bed on fire. I reasoned with him, reluctant to turn him in, but to no effect. Bad smokers with these habits usually were chased off the Mid Canada line but this offender had managed to cover up his activities with suitable gifts to the room attendant who, on at least two occasions, threw fire-damaged mattresses on the dump and drew new ones without reporting the incidents.

Then one night, the inevitable happened. The smoker, in an alcoholic daze, suffered severe shoulder burns before the fire was discovered. He was so far along he never knew he was hurt, or had been treated, until he sobered up. He went, but there was something about Byrd that lingered. It wasn't a happy station.

The service posting term to this God-forsaken area was long enough for some of the less stable, military and civilians, to get shack happy. This was a real problem on the Dew Line and I have been required, on more than one occasion, to fly out mentally-fatigued technicians from the radar posts to see what treatment, rest and recreation could do for them.

A lot of the lads were there with the idea of saving their admittedly excellent salaries and hurrying back to the little woman with a sizeable stake when their term ended. It isn't a bad idea, if you have the proper temperament to stick to it, but it wasn't everyone's dish of coffee.

Then there was the problem of the 'Dear John' letters,

137

messages from wives and sweethearts who wrote from the U.S. that they had found their true love and the outposted hero had better not plan on returning to a domestic nest now dismantled.

I was told that the U.S. military machine was careful to examine the real condition on the home site to determine if the sentiments were genuine. There were occasions when such letters were in response to signals from Greenland conveyed in letter code that activated the letter writing, for in many cases the stricken male would be sent home to try to salvage his marriage. The compassionate grounds escape hatch could be, and was, used to this end. In peace time, I suspected, men in uniform have even more time to figure out ways to beat the system than during a war. The compensating factor, of course, may be that the brass and the flunkeys also have more time to devise ways to stop the troops from cheating.

The lucky ones at Sondrestrom were the Globemaster crews. They were rotated every two weeks. During their term in Greenland they were in a state of constant readiness, the planes' engines and control instruments kept warmed at all times, so that they could be airborne in less than three minutes.

They had periodic test alerts, although they never could be sure they were tests and had to react as if they were the real thing, a condition that led to a few comical situations such as the occasion when the hooter sounded and crews came pouring out of various nooks and crannies. Leading them was an officer, stark naked, who had been taking a shower. He carried his flying boots in one hand and his uniform in the other, figuring he could dress when his plane was airborne.

This sort of drill, and two-week rotations, kept the crews sharp and provided them with air time they might not otherwise have had. It was all very impressive, even to an old R.C.A.F. type. It was only when my expanding taxpayer's status reasserted itself that I flinched at the cost.

Although we flew almost everything into Dye-One the main fuel supply for the area came in once a year by tanker. This usually arrived following an icebreaker. It would tie up at the base of the mountain site at Dye-One and pump fuel ashore where it was moved by pipeline to the site above. Heavy equipment also came in by sea and was moved to the site along a crude 13 miles long mountain road.

Sondrestrom was completely equipped and self-sustaining once supplies had arrived. There was a splendidly equipped hospital. Five different clubs catered to the entertainment of the officers and airmen. The newest films were flown in for regular showing. The clubs had bowling alleys and slot machines in profusion.

There were 19 slots in the officers' club which had, as well, a complete gaming room with roulette and black jack, the whole shot. It was like Las Vegas, except that the slots were rigged to return a better payoff.

The sergeants had the same sort of setup, perhaps even better. Sergeants and warrant officers seem to be in that position in most services. They actually owned their own club, paying for it with the proceeds of the games. It was worth about a million dollars and was fitted up with a fine dining room, a magnificent bar and the other assets of a first-class night spot.

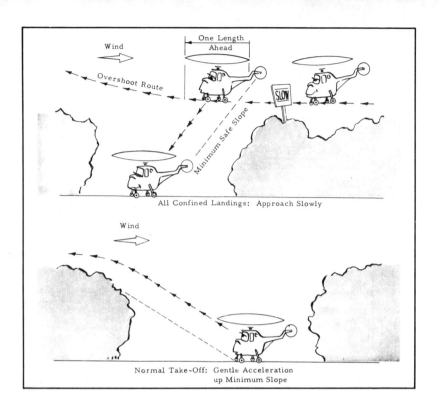

All Confined Landings: Approach Slowly

Normal Take-Off: Gentle Acceleration
up Minimum Slope

140

# 9

# The General Goes Fishing

A flyer learns never to be surprised but I must confess I was astonished, one morning in July, 1961, to find myself fishing some of the numerous Greenland lakes near a well-known U.S. strategic air base, in company with the commander of U.S. Strategic Air Command and some of his top brass.

It was, in a way, an unexpected culmination of a five-month tour of chopper duty that had begun the previous March. I hadn't joined the U.S. air force, of course, but I found myself in Greenland because my employers at that praticular moment, Kenting Helicopters of Toronto, had contracted to provide choppers and pilots for SAC and the authorities handling (DEW) Line radar stations in that area.

I was based at Sondrestrom, on the west coast of Greenland about one-third of the way up that island.

The fishing excursion hit us one summer's day when a full colonel flew in out of the blue and informed us that General Lawrence Kuter, and some lesser lights, would arrive at Sondrestrom the following morning for an 'inspection' of the base. His questions and orders made it clear that the real reason for the visit was the General's desire to try the fishing.

Kuter, top hand at SAC, was a five-star general, an imperious figure in the military hierarchy  His advance man was there to see that everything fell into place for the visit.

141

He asked me if my choppers had floats. I had to tell him we had floats but they had not been installed and we were using wheels (which I don't like) and that the time element made it impossible for the two Kenting civilian engineers to install the floats in time for the fishing trip.

This was no obstacle to the emissary of the American proconsul. He said that the floats were vital because we would be flying mostly over water and he proceeded to order up a work party of two dozen American service men who worked all night replacing the wheels with the floats. The latter won't wear as well as wheels but they offer a big plus in safety.

The next day Kuter arrived on time, almost to the second. There was no delay as we loaded the two rented Canadian choppers with U.S. air force brass and flew off down the fiord where a 65-foot launch was waiting. It was a luxury setup, complete with chef, bar and most of the creature comforts of a resort hotel, and we went out fishing in the same well-ordered manner.

As we hummed along from the base to the launch I was stunned to see a large Albatross airplane flying cover for us. I was told that it was there to relay messages of an urgent nature that might not reach us flying among the mountain fiords. I was impressed. The Americans seemed to have thought of everything and it shook me a bit to think that if Doomsday arrived I would be one of the first to know. I confess that it was ego-flattering to think that for several hours I was a key link in the chain of SAC command, for I was my own wireless operator in the helicopter.

The fishing was excellent, so good in fact that we soon had a large catch and the visitors were beginning to weary of reeling in the fine trout that swarmed in the lakes. It was time to knock off for a drink and a lunch of the fish we caught, handsomely presented by the launch crew. After the meal Kuter decided that he had had enough fishing and asked to be flown to a DEW line post.

My special servicing responsibility was on a remote mountain station on top of a 5200-foot eminence about 65 miles west of Sondrestrom. As we headed for Dye-One my wireless set began to make noises and I was told the

142

Albatross had an urgent message for the general.

Naturally I was excited but being at the center of communications as well as being captain of the chopper offered a few problems. To fly a chopper you have two controls to work with your hands, as I have explained. One of them, the collective, on the left side, can be locked into position, something I quickly did. But the cyclic had to be managed by putting it between my knees and hoping for the best while I laboriously wrote down the urgent message on an official message pad as Kuter, in the seat beside me, peeked over to see what it was all about.

The earth-shaking communication was a stunner. It was a query from the U.S. base at Goose Bay, Newfoundland, asking for instructions about the order of dress to be worn by officers when Kuter took dinner with them on his way back from Sondrestrom. I handed the general the message pad. His face darkened as he read it. "Tell them I don't give a damn what they wear," he growled.

Later I had a few moments of silent sorrow for the poor old U.S. taxpayer stuck with the bills for two helicopters and pilots, a 65-foot launch, an Albatross, the giant jet in which the general travelled, the services of 24 men changing the choppers over to floats, and the cost of transporting all that brass to Greenland for a morning's fishing.

The monstrous ice wall was still growling and appeared likely to undergo another collapse. We had to work swiftly and opened a shuttle service to lift out the dead and the living. I was astonished to find that most of the men had never ridden in a helicopter. Several were so stricken by the trauma of the event that they were unwilling to get aboard and had to be forced to enter the chopper cabin.

My admiration for American ingenuity in a crisis rose when I noticed that by the time I had returned with my first load of wounded, all the wires in the front of the hospital, along with other obstacles, had been cleared away to make an emergency landing pad right in front of the building. That same afternoon, after receiving emergency treatment, those who could be moved were loaded on a Globemaster and flown back to hospitals in the U.S.

It was a catastrophe that had never happened before and

143

will never happen again at Sondrestrom for today servicemen are closely supervised in any visits to the glacier and kept more distant from it and beyond the reach of the ice field's anger.

One of the dead men had arrived in Greenland only three days before the mishap. His was a particularly sad case for he had been married only the weekend prior to his departure for the posting. Fatalists would say it just happened to be the day his number came up.

Sondrestrom is so remote that some of the personnel are inclined to feel that the strict rules of safety enforced on such bases is a bit more than necessary. There were full medical staffs and crash crews on the long single-strip airfield at all times and sternly-enforced rules against smoking. We were not permitted to refuel until a crash tender had been positioned nearby in case of fire. Well, I had never had a fire in my lengthening career and thought it a bit ridiculous to have the fire truck and its spray nozzle pointed at me every time my chopper took on fuel. I knew, naturally, the danger of fire from static electricity in cold climates, one reason why nylon and synthetic fibre clothing is not permitted around an airfield, but I felt my understanding of safety was more than adequate.

Or I did until one day when the virtue of the foam nozzle was demonstrated in vivid fashion just after a chopper had landed not far from mine. The pilot didn't get out but sat in the cockpit writing up his log. Suddenly all hell broke loose. To explain what happened I must mention that for lift-off and landing a chopper pilot uses both an engine-driven fuel pump and an electrically-driven backup pump. On takeoff you turn on your electric pump until airborne, and you reactivate it when coming down to land.

In this case the pilot had activated his backup pump when setting down but had forgotten to switch it off. When he shut off his master switches the backup stopped and because everything was quiet he didn't realize the switch was still on. As he sat writing his engineer began to pump fuel into the side of the chopper into the tank opening located slightly ahead of the open cargo door. Only a few feet away the foam

144

gun looked down at the machine from the top of the fire truck.

The fuel hose, a high pressure device, quickly began to fill the tank and the engineer, uncertain how much gas was required, shouted to the pilot through the open cockpit door and asked if enough fuel had been loaded.

The pilot gestured for the engineer to wait, reached over and switched on the master switch to activate the fuel gauge. The forgotten backup pump under the floorboards of the main cabin was activated by the turn of the switch. Unfortunately that was all that was needed. Fumes from the fuel had entered the region of the pump and in a split second the helicopter exploded into flames. The engineer, startled by this turn of events, instinctively leaped away from the flames. As he did so his grip tightened on the fuel hose control, squirting gasoline into the interior of the cargo cabin. The pilot, abandoning his log book, bailed out of the cockpit. Both men could have been burned to a cinder but for the instant response of the fireman manning the foam nozzle. In seconds he had the chopper and the area around it covered with several feet of foam, a massive application that snuffed out the fire with a minimum of damage.

The pilot was doubly lucky. When he bailed out he landed on his head on the packed tarmac, fortunately he hadn't bothered to remove his crash helmet.

Some of the safety rules probably seem as silly and unnessary today as they did then. All I can say is that they may continually surprise people with their importance if they are applied in the specific circumstance they were drafted to cover.

Once a week the club operators put on 'loss leaders,' martinis for a dime, Manhattans for the same price; and you could drink your fill for an hour or so until the regular prices came back. Every once in a while the club tossed a free dinner for its members. Normally you paid but the prices were ridiculous: a dollar for lobster tails with butter.

Champagne, good stuff, too, was a dollar a bottle, a price that led to the invention of a game in which the imbibers became marksmen ricocheting champagne corks off the ceiling at selected targets, for side bets. The Americans, I

145

soon realized, weren't opposed to Demon Rum but had signed him on as an ally to fight Saucy Sex, or whatever comes from the lack of it.

The base exchange, totally free of taxes, was a delight for post shoppers who could pick up things like expensive cameras and watches for about 40% of their U.S. retail price. The best booze cost $2.00 for 40 oz.—no limit at Sondrestrom.

Men at this outpost had lots of time for meditation and some of it led to startling conclusions. There was my friend Al, station chief at Dye-One who was pondering a family problem. He had been informed that it would be unwise for his wife to have any more children. Al, a kindly sort, decided that he could solve the problem for her during his incarceration on the DEW Line. He filed a formal request for the Sondrestrom medics to send out a doctor to perform a vasectomy on him. It was his idea that this would make the finest kind of homecoming surprise.

The U.S. government was willing, so in due time I was instructed to fly a doctor out to the radar base where the relatively simple operation was quickly performed, somewhere in the bowels of the establishment. That seemed the end to Mr. and Mrs. Al's worries about unwanted pregnancies, and at no cost, for the medical treatment was free, part of the enlistment contract.

As so often is the case, this example of the course of true love and the devotion of lovers turned out to be much more than planned. A few days later there was an emergency call from Dye-One where I found Al doubled up in great agony. I flew him out to Sondrestrom where the docs discovered that an infection had set in.

He had somewhat more than a temperature, for his private parts had assumed the size of a pair of prize melons, making it almost impossible for him to walk.

His condition impressed even his best friends. As he wrestled with his problem Al was sitting in my room with me and Brian Hayter, and we were commiserating with him when one of his closest buddies looked in, spotted Al and asked, "What the hell are you doing here?"

As Al struggled to put his answer in not-too-painful terms

146

Brian interjected. "Oh," he offered brightly, "he's got an infection in his testicles. Why, one's the size of a football, and the other's a really great big bastard."

It was quite some time before things returned to normal. Whether Mrs. Al ever really learned how much her husband had gone through for her sake isn't clear.

During my five-month stay in Sondrestrom I was involved in a genuine tragedy in which four airmen were killed. It was one of those unpredictable things that makes men into fatalists for the victims were members of a busload of off-duty men engaged in an innocent diversion.

They had been taken out to have a close-up look at Greenland's eternal glacier, driving some 12 miles to the general vicinity of the glacier wall where they got out and walked to an icy river running from the melting walls of the awe-inspiring spectacle.

The glacier towered 600 or 700 feet into the air. It was blue, and it seemed almost alive, filling the air with strange rumblings.

As the visitors stood talking and taking pictures of this truly impressive work of nature, the wall of the glacier suddenly collapsed; exploded is a better word, showering the adjacent river and land with huge blocks of ice hurled around like sugar cubes tossed by giants.

The stunned onlookers had no time to move as the great blocks of ice ran over and through them. The terrible projectiles killed four men outright and seriously injured a dozen more. The victims lay strewn around like soldiers caught in an ambush on some forlorn battlefield.

By a stroke of chance I and the other civilian chopper pilot weren't flying that day. We were sunning ourselves when a man, almost hysterical, ran up shouting words of the tragedy. He had run the 12 miles back to the station as he could not start the bus. The alarm sounded and within minutes we had our choppers en route to the glacier area.

My first helicopter assignment was to fly Assistant District Commissioner Mike Foley and some other officials into an interior mountain village. Most of these settlements had no road connections and the airplane or helicopter was the only

147

link to them except for arduous week-long treks through the jungle.

Most had no airfields and the chopper was by far the easiest way to get into them for, in the long, slow development of communal life, the huts in which the natives lived had come to surround a sizeable open area that served them as a community meeting place, and now became an excellent landing pad for 'copters.

I had been given a hurried briefing on where and how to land, and warned that the noise of my machine would alert the natives and they would be assembled in large numbers as we came in. Sure enough, as we approached the village several hundred people were ringing the landing zone. I came down very carefully for I was not sure of how they would react and my worst fears seemed justified when one of the older men dashed forward from the mass of spectators screaming and waving a large axe.

No one had warned me that this was a form of official greeting so I decided to play it cautiously. I poured on the coal and lifted off again, circling the village like a coyote sniffing a baited trap. My companions reassured me, saying there really was no danger. This time I flew the chopper into a long approach path that automatically chased the people to the sides. I saw no more of the man with the axe.

The natives usually stayed well clear of aircraft, which they regarded with awe despite the hundreds of machines they had seen during the Second World War action that encompassed their area. For many, I have been told, memories of the temporary 1941-45 visitations are now blurred and at least one religious sect has made some converts preaching a doctrine that proclaims: gods in airborne machines will arrive and bring endless showers of rewards to all true believers. Naturally the natives who had settled in the towns knew better than that, certainly enough to regard with suspicion any claim that flying ships shower gifts.

New Guinea natives are a polyglot. They speak scores of languages which vary in such a marked degree that a village sometimes cannot communicate with its closest neighbor. Some tribes are small physically, the largest members not

148

much over four feet tall. Others are large and beautifully muscled.

It is a colonial society, even in the towns in what we like to think of as the civilized areas. In the remote regions the populace relies on hard-working district commissioners of the Kipling, Somerset Maugham school. These men, dedicated to their work, tend to the health, community needs and safeguarding of the natives and their interests. They work hard, sometimes on distasteful assignments including the periodic checks for leprosy for which I acted as pilot.

These native people are intelligent and, with a little training, can fit into a variety of roles in the towns, as truck drivers, policemen, and, where education is available and some patience shown, they have demonstrated their ability to handle skilled tradesmen's jobs.

In the forest wilderness I found that the people suffer physically from an unvaried diet based on sweet potatoes. They eat little meat or fish, and their food intake is seriously unbalanced by western standards. Like many other inhabitants of the tropics they chew betel nuts, a habit that stains their mouths red. The betel seems to provide some sort of glow, a high not unlike that produced by alcohol in the western world. As do folk of many other races, the New Guineans love to gamble, so much, in fact, that the use of playing cards has been banned. In their simple society arguments about card games frequently resulted in death or injury, and started tribal blood feuds.

Christian missionaries have worked in the area for several generations, coming from Germany, Australia, the U.S., Canada and other Christian countries. They have had what I would term 'fair success' in converting the natives but there is some reason to believe that many of the converts are typical 'rice Christians'. Certainly Christianity strikes one as a veneer for they still pay their respects to the tribal witch doctors and believe in the spirits of nature and other superstitions.

Periodically tribal wars erupted, often for what might be considered trivial reasons. The Australian authorities are quick to react because these flare-ups can spread quickly and widely if not stamped out immediately.

149

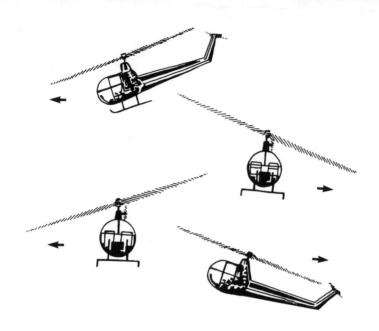

# 10

# Back to the Stone Age

My company had some crews working in Australia, attracted, no doubt, by the lure of faraway places and the big money that goes to specialists working overseas. On closer examination, for quite a few of them, the attraction soon lost its luster. More than a few, in fact, just couldn't adjust to being that far from home, in many cases separated from their families in long, lonely months of apartness that can do more damage to people's health than the bubonic plague. Rotation might have helped, but the company couldn't meet the expense of moving personnel back and forth 12,000 miles, or of moving families with school children to the other side of the world for a relatively brief period.

As a result it was hard to keep people Down Under and in December, 1964, word reached me up in Cornerbrook that there were openings in Australia and that the company had a job there for me if I wanted it.

Inge and I talked it over and decided that we would like to have a look at that part of the world. We had no children, and it wouldn't hurt to ask. So I telephoned my boss, Neil Armstrong, at the Ottawa headquarters. He explained that it was a short-term posting, perhaps only for a few weeks, and that no wives or families would be going. That seemed to settle it—we had decided to go together or not at all. Expecting to be in Newfoundland for the whole winter, we

151

found an empty apartment in Cornerbrook, filled it with new furniture including a stove and fridge, and sat back to wait for Spring.

A couple of weeks later Armstrong called to say that he had received a cable from Helicopter Utilities in Sydney asking if he knew of any pilots available on short notice. He gave me the telephone number and once more things were all up in the air.

This time we decided to go. I picked up the telephone and called Sydney and very quickly found myself talking to Ken Hammond, operations manager of Helicopter Utilities. I thought he sounded a bit sunstruck and wondered about it until he explained that it was two o'clock in the morning for him and I had roused him from a deep sleep.

After we talked a bit and I told him about myself he wanted me to come right away, along with my wife. I told him it was no go; that we needed two weeks. He agreed to wait, and in a couple of days we had sold back our furniture to the dealer from whom we had bought it, a deal costing us only a modest $200 on the exchange.

Two weeks later, after holidaying stops across the Pacific, we walked down the ramp at Sydney airport. The long trip had been a saga of frustrating delays and demonstrations of incompetence and we were pleased at last to step into noonday sunlight and a greeting by operations manager Ken Hammond. He had no trouble picking us out of the dozen or so passengers in the lightly loaded plane because Inge was carrying her fur coat. The airport thermometer read 96 in the shade. We had experienced 124 degrees of temperature change since leaving Newfoundland.

"Welcome to Australia," said Ken with a friendly grin. "I trust you had a comfortable journey. I have arranged for your medical and written examination for your Australian commercial pilot's licence this afternoon," he told me.

"Thank you, but no thanks," I replied. "I'm so bushed I doubt if I could pass water, let alone an exam."

He took us directly to our quarters at Bankstown airport and it was 48 hours later that I tried and passed those examinations, and in 72 hours more I was on my new assignment in New Guinea, leaving Inge in a single bedroom seaside apartment for the month I would need to find accommodation for her in the unknown land in which we were destined to spend the next two years.

There is a time machine feeling for any Canadian visiting New Guinea-Papua. I know, I experienced it. I had moved through 13,000 air miles by the time I reached the Protectorate which occupies the eastern half of the island. I realized that I had gone back as many years in time, when I visited the native villages. They are inhabited by tribes still in the Stone Age from which they are being hauled out of by events such as the Second World War and the changes brought by the uneasy peace since 1945.

The natives of New Guinea know little of our affluence. They certainly haven't shared in it to any noticeable extent. In the remotest villages life is altering only slowly but the change seems inescapable.

My first visit to a native village was a startling experience for which I was totally unprepared despite my contact with the Indian and Eskimo peoples of Canada's Northland. It came soon after I travelled from Sydney to Port Moresby on an Ansett A.N.A. Australian Airlines plane, then, by DC-3, on to Mt. Hagen, a community created in the mountains some 5500 feet above sea level by the former German rulers of this area, and taken from them in the 1919 Treaty of Versailles.

Some of the control methods would offend the Civil Liberties Union, I'm sure. One district commissioner told me how he put an end to a growing tribal feud by sending in a patrol of six native policemen armed with rifles. They speedily stopped the trouble by shooting three men held to be the ringleaders.

Unfortunately, in their own land the New Guineans are regarded as second-rate citizens. They were treated in hospitals that were disgraceful, many of them with dirt floors, a minimum of treatment facilities and a few drugs or medicines. It was a shocking contrast to the modern hospitals open to the white population in the same community.

As a result, the village people are reluctant to go to any hospital for they equate hospital treatment with the final

153

stage of life before death. Because they believe that few come out alive, they shy away from seeking treatment for illnesses and injuries until their condition has become desperate. Many are *in extremis* by the time they arrive and their fear of hospitals becomes a self-fulfilling prophecy. I flew many patients to hospital and this terror was obvious.

Some, seriously ill but still ambulant, would bolt into the forest when the resident missionary told them they had to go away for treatment. On more than one occasion I have flown into villages to pick up patients and found they had fled on the sound of my approach.

Upgrading the lot of the natives is no easy task, although some honest effort has been made. Plans have been instituted to improve their diet by setting up cattle ranch operations and special ventures into fisheries. Only in a few cases has there been success. Attempts to initiate rice growing and sheep farming have also been ineffective.

The valleys of that mountainous land hold many lakes. One of my jobs was to seed them with fish that could be used as food. It was the personal project of a district commissioner who created a sizeable fish-rearing pond near his headquarters in which he raised fish from the egg stage.

When the fingerlings were large enough I carried them in water-filled plastic containers and put them into the lakes. Air seeding of lakes has worked well in Canada but I don't know what the result has been in New Guinea.

In an effort to establish a cottage industry some villagers were instructed in the cultivation of the pyrethrum plant, the flowers of which, when dried and powdered, form the base of several insecticides.

In spite of these efforts, the country continues to rely on its old standbys, placer mining of gold (the best claims are worked out), lumbering in the quick-growth tropical hardwood forests, coffee growing, peanut farming and copra production.

It is largely an agricultural society but one that lives close to the modern world and uses and requires the services of motor vehicles and airplanes.

I was surprised at the extent of the coffee plantations and the quality of the product. There were 44 plantations around

154

Mount Hagen, most of them planted during the period before the First World War when Germany ran the colony.

New Guinea, of course, is the traditional home of cannibal tribes with traditions and customs that may still be maintained in the remotest areas, although they had been eliminated in any of the villages I visited. Whether there is secret backsliding this far along in the 20th century is a subject of debate. The authorities, in any event, keep close enough watch to make it highly unlikely.

The district commissioners and the patrol officers working under them, as I have noted, are single-minded men, totally devoted to their jobs, whose existence in the remoter parts of the land seems to be some form of self-inflicted punishment. Deep in the wilderness I got to know one such patrol officer whose job required him to make a circuit of many miles of deep jungle territory on trips that would keep him away for several weeks at a time.

The helicopter was a godsend to him for I was able to lift him and his supplies 35 miles to the starting point of one long-range patrol. It is difficult to imagine what it was like. I like comparing it to Stanley's setting out to find Livingstone. There was nearly a ton of food and supplies to be moved through the jungle, goods packed into bundles just large enough to be portable by each of the 40 native bearers whom I had flown in to accompany the officer.

Even the fantastic beauty of the land cannot compensate for the difficulties of having to move across it on foot. It must do something to the white man, for this particular representative of law-and-order clearly was suffering from some deep-seated *malais*.

We were billeted in the residence of a schoolteacher who was on sabbatical. The poor soul probably needed the rest, for the place was infested with some of the biggest cockroaches I have ever seen or heard about, up to two inches long, as fearless as they were large. Cockroaches have survived, without evolutionary change, for millions of years, possibly because people find them so revolting they can't move to deal with them permanently, or have given up the task as impossible.

Cockroaches, however, are only one of a myriad forms of

155

insect and animal life in New Guinea, a country with some 70 varieties of snakes.

Inge, who had joined me after spending a month acquiring a deep sun tan on the Australian beaches, was perpetually fascinated by the geckoes, small nocturnal lizards having adhesive pads on their feet which allow them to scurry up walls and even across smooth ceilings.

They are something out of believe-it-or-not, almost translucent with a tail which will break off in your fingers if you attempt to pick one up. The gecko with his stump scuttles away into sulky isolation and grows a replacement. Geckoes are not only harmless but useful for they prey on flies and other insects. Despite their numbers they never seem to dirty a place for there is no sign of their droppings. Perhaps they have a gecko bathroom hidden away in the roofs of the buildings they inhabit.

When I started to work with Helicopter Utilities I was assured that I would be given a permanent posting that would permit Inge and me to maintain a home in one place. It was a come-on, I soon found. After she joined me in Mount Hagen, I had to charter a Cessna 180 to fly her in from Lae. We moved constantly and actually lived out of our suitcases for seven straight months.

Utilities was working under a charter to the Australian government, at expensive rates, a fact that astounded me more than a little after I received my parting advice on leaving Sydney. "Don't fly unless you have to," I was told. I discovered that the charter provided Utilities with a daily fee for the helicopter and pilot whether there was any actual use of them or not. Keeping the chopper grounded meant that the cost of maintenance from wear-and-tear would be reduced without any reduction in return.

So we moved around on short-term assignments that took us to Lae, Goroka, Port Moresby, Madang, Wewak and many more locations. It might mean a week or two in one place, or a day or two in another, but for a time we looked forward to the changes because we wanted to see as much of this strange land and its people as we could.

Our circle of friends and acquaintances continued to widen as we became acclimatized. One of our new associates was Dave Marsh, the district commissioner at Mendi, a perfect host, delightful conversationalist and friend who maintained a small, separate apartment just to entertain guests like us. Dave was the conscientious official who developed the fish-stocking program. He worked desperately hard in the 20-odd years he had been in New Guinea, a concerned servant who illumined the ranks of the civil servants and contributed so much to the well-being of the New Guineans.

On one of our trips to a native village I took Inge along to feel the vibrations of life at that level. I thought the village missionary was a bit cool in his welcome but we didn't discover why until later. Inge was wearing shorts, something she does very well. But in native villages, the writ reads, white women do not go around with their limbs exposed. Thereafter Inge wore slacks. She also learned that it was important to have an escort for any visit to an area outside the white section of any community.

We were at Goroka when I had a brush with disaster that gave me a scare. Perhaps these are necessary from time to time, for they work against slackness. Pilots in the jungle are exceptionally careful for even if they come down safely there is no certainty that they can be found in the massive rain forests.

On this day, while airborne, I felt severe vibrations on the rudder pedals when some 30 miles from base. I called Madang on my radio, told them where I was, where I was heading, and kept calling them every 10 minutes with up-dated information. My machine seemed to vibrate more with each passing minute. I could do nothing but nurse it along and hope that by some miracle it would hold together. Somehow or other it did. How I can't imagine, for when I put it down at Goroka I discovered that the main tail rotor bearing had disintegrated.

I didn't have long to sweat about it. We were too busy and after that sort of thing it is well for one's peace of mind to have as little time as possible to reflect. My main problem was getting new parts, which had to be flown in from Australia.

Inge and I were still hopping around like witch doctors at a

157

tribal ceremony and becoming somewhat tired of it. I conveyed our feelings to head office and, as usual, there were plenty of soothing words and, when pressed, a promise of a permanent posting at Lae.

All my experience warned me to take this assurance with reservations but I began to believe that it must be true for I was ordered to report to Lae almost at once. It is one of the largest and most comfortable communities in that whole remote land, located on the coast and commanding a spectacular view of the beautiful blue Pacific. We were certain we would love it there.

Things went swimmingly at first. I went into the weekly newspaper office to insert an ad for a house. The editor-business manager assured me none was available but consented to run the ad, having done his duty in warning me that I was wasting my money.

Within a couple of hours he came to see me. "The most amazing thing has happened," he said. "After you left a man came in and said he wanted to put an ad offering a house for rent. I haven't seen anything like it in years."

This amiable man 'married up' his two potential advertisers. We made a deal on the spot, the marriage broker losing his fees but earning the deep gratitude of both erstwhile clients.

Soon after Inge and I settled in we met a man named Crowley, owner of an airline of the same name. He told me he had a fleet of conventional planes but was expecting two helicopters to augment his fleet, and suggested I might be interested in joining his company. The point was not pressed when I did not respond and I thought no more of it until a few days later when, out of the blue, Utilities ordered me to Port Moresby for a posting to Daru, a remote and unattractive post, for an undetermined period.

I telephoned Sydney, charged management with a breach of promise, and was firmly informed I had to go, and that the instruction was an order. I walked out of the office determined not to go. I telephoned Lae and told Crowley I was available. He seemed delighted, saying he would give me a job flying fixed-wing planes until the helicopters arrived.

Determined to have nothing more to do with Utilities, I

158

booked a flight to Lae on a commercial airliner, leaving my chopper on the Port Moresby airfield. I still don't understand what the fuss was all about for Utilities didn't even bother to retrieve it for about six weeks.

My service with the company that had lured me Down Under ended with mixed feelings on my part, and a store of good memories, among them the occasion on which I played air chauffeur to a man I have long admired, Admiral of the Fleet, Earl Mountbatten of Burma, K.G., P.C., G.C.B., G.C.S.I., G.C.V.O., D.S.O., D.C.L., D.Sc. Quite a string of decorations but none too many for an unstuffy, thoroughly capable and likable individual, one of the few remaining Allied Leaders of the Second World War. Mountbatten has achieved distinction, rising to play a truly useful role in international affairs. He is widely respected throughout the former lands of the British Empire, so it was an occasion of consequence and a matter of pride to all of us when he visited New Guinea in 1964.

Inge and I were living at Mt. Hagen when Mountbatten arrived to open a spanking new airport that would replace the small, dangerous landing strip in the center of the town.

A tremendous amount of planning had been put into arranging the visit. The natives had been alerted for miles around, and on the big day upwards of 70,000 of them had assembled to greet him.

The New Guineans poured into Mt. Hagen in full tribal regalia, the men armed with spears and shields, the historic weapons of the tribes. They were ornamented with paint, and wore huge feather headdresses of Bird of Paradise feathers. It was a scene out of Cecil B. DeMille. I'm sure it exited Mountbatten as much as it did Inge and me to see some 70,000 natives welcome the distinguished guest to their land in a pageant of dances, mock war charges, singing and celebration.

Aircraft flew in from all over the territory and staged an air show. As the only helicopter pilot I found myself front and center, demonstrating the versatility of this important communications item in that mountainous land.

Later I flew Mountbatten and district commissioner Tom Ellis to Banz and Nondugal, dropping down frequently to give them close-up views of the jungle and the native villages.

At Nondugal, Mountbatten was entranced by a visit to the spectacular Bird of Paradise sanctuary where these magnificent animals display the color and spread of a plumage that is a global byword for the spectacular in adornment. This lovely resident of New Guinea now is protected by law, a recognition that too fine feathers can make for extinction of the species. Mountbatten clearly was interested. His conversation was lively and his questions pertinent.

His visit wound up in another breath of vanished empire, a garden party at Mt. Hagen on the final evening, with more than 600 guests. It was a scene lighted by scores of lanterns shining on dress uniforms and elegant gowns, huge tables loaded with a superb buffet, with music, and formal courtesy of the old, and not dishonorable days of colonial rule.

For those few hours Mountbatten was a sparkling throwback to the great proconsuls of the past, but as he departed to resume his role in London as Chief of the Defence Staff, he once more became the soldier-scientist-sailor-author of wide-ranging modern accomplishment.

On his return flight to Whitehall he took time out to write me a gracious note thanking me for my services, in which he expressed his conviction that the helicopter will play a vital role in the development of the territories.

# 11
# Jungle Pilot

One of the best places to live in New Guinea has to be Lae, in 1965 a town of about 5000 evenly divided in numbers between natives and whites, where District Commissioner A.T. Timperley was the presiding civil servant. Inge and I certainly had a most favorable immediate impression of Lae. Later we were to learn that the physical beauty of the place was only one side of the coin; some other aspects of life there were not nearly so attractive.

The town is about three-quarters of the way up the east coast of what was until recently an Australian protectorate, and in 1965 it was a relatively new community built to replace one almost completely destroyed during the Second World War. The only building left from those hectic days was a complex of Nissen huts to which several additions had been made to enable them to serve as a post office-municipal center.

Lae is at the mouth of the Markham River, one of the largest of the island's many waterways, and is the center of a prosperous agricultural area dotted with tea and coffee plantations and fine vegetable farms. It is set in a region that features a growing lumber industry in which klinkii pine plywood is an important product.

The town also provides access to the Norobe gold field around Wau, an inland village some 50 miles to the

161

southeast, where, for many years, gold was extracted with large dredges. By the time we arrived the alluvial workings had been washed several times and only one dredge remained. The new Lae has been erected on a terrace back from the ocean where the river debouches into the salt water, and most of it overlooks the old airfield and offers a wide seascape.

Here our personal effects, shipped months before by ocean freighter, finally caught up with us. We almost wished they hadn't for we found them scattered all over the dock, the contents damaged and strewn around. The picture tube on the TV set was in splinters. Our pictures were ruined and some valuable and cherished furniture was scarred and broken. Despite the damage we could not collect a penny in insurance for the shipping company alleged the goods were improperly packed, although we had paid a professional mover to look after them.

What survived helped furnish a two-bedroom house provided by Crowley, a comfortable residence on a 140- by 160-foot lot. It was blessed with a magnificent tropical garden with all kinds of fruits, including figs and pineapples, and gorgeous tropical plants and flowers. The layout was tended five days weekly by a native gardener to whom I paid the princely wage of one Australian pound ($2.57 Canadian, then) for the week. I thought it was scandalously low and said so but was warned not to pay more as it was the going rate and to alter it would rock the boat for everyone else.

Native servants were plentiful and similarly poorly paid. Most of them were reasonably competent and honest. Our gardener, Liagram, had good references and lived up to them, which was not always the case, we were told. Examples were cited of natives who came with good references bought or borrowed for the occasion in the belief, seemingly justified, that whites cannot tell one native from anot'
For all its beauty, Lae was an uneasy place for whites. Inge was warned not to go around unescorted because too many careless females had been robbed, raped and even murdered. One victim, killed about the time we arrived, was the wife of an Australian serviceman, who was attacked while bathing at the beach. Many of the white families had firearms and,

162

because I would be away from home a great deal, I took their advice and obtained a police permit to buy a small pistol for Inge.

On one occasion when I was away overnight Ingeborg was awakened by a noise on the verandah. There is only fly screen covering the windows—no glass—so entry to a home is very easy. She phoned the police, who arrived in minutes. They searched the area and found only our garden boy, who apparently was asleep in his quarters at the back of the yard. He could not convince them that he was innocent of any wrongdoing. They took him to the police station and kept him until noon next day and only released him on the insistence of Ingeborg that he was not guilty.

The white Inspector asked Ingeborg if she had a pistol and she assured him she had. "Shoot first and we'll ask questions later," he advised her. Fortunately she never had occasion to put this advice into use.

The house that now was our home was a tropical veteran, its years obvious in the ancient fans, suspended from the ceiling, that rotated in slow, stately, sometimes creaky fashion, and reminded us of movies about tropical outposts of the empire and Saunders of the River occasions. We painted the interior and soon were much more comfortable than we could have been in any local hotel.

I had my own experience with one of these establishments. At the Cecil, the largest hotel, I was told I would not need a key. My room, I found, was multi-residential, with five single cots, and when I awoke the next day I found I was sharing the cramped space with four absolute strangers, unfortunately all males!

For a time at least I also had a very ancient jeep, provided by Crowley to carry me to and from the airfield. It was a Second World War relic, bearing grim scars of age and hard usage. It looked near the end of its career, and so it proved. One day, as Inge and I rode in it, a cloud of smoke rolled up from the floorboards. Within seconds flames were licking at its battered frame. We jumped out and I ran to a nearby store and asked the native owner if I could use his telephone to call the fire department. He said I could if I gave him 10 cents, the amount I would have had to pay to use a public telephone call box. I was prepared to pay but had no change. The storekeeper couldn't change a bill. While we bickered and argued the jeep burned down to its tires.

We had to have transportation so we bought a Volkswagen of more recent vintage which Inge enjoyed driving when I was away. On one occasion she ran over an eight-foot snake sunning itself on the dirt road. It startled her but not enough to make her get out to identify the species. On another trip she put a sizable dent in the front left fender. Weighed down with the prospect of confessing her difficulty she had the bright idea of hurrying the 'bug' to a panel-beating shop where a smiling native pounded out the dent and touched it up with fresh paint, all for $5, and did it so well that I didn't notice it until some time later when she told me about her accident. Five-buck repair jobs are fiction in North America and may well have vanished in New Guinea by this time.

Lae was, and still is, an aviation center. There are some 20 deserted airstrips in the Markham Valley, wartime leftovers for the most part and so close together that I still can't imagine that all of them were used at the same time. Towards the end of our stay they started rebuilding one of them to accommodate jet fighters of the Royal Australian Air Force.

Crowley had a fleet of 12 fixed-wing planes that I flew for three months until the two helicopters arrived. Thereafter I handled both choppers and conventionals, a two-way stretch that pleased Crowley who was a rare task-master anxious to keep people busy from morning to night.

He was a driver, as hard as any I have known, and a shrewd businessman withal. He had us hauling coffee beans from the plantations, hundreds of tons of them, and some from a plantation that he owned that were carried to Lae to be processed in the Crowley plant there.

My New Guinea service gave me a rare opportunity to observe the natives and their hundreds of tribes. In the Mendi district alone, for example, there were 600 tribal families. Their customs were strange to us, exotic, even a little sinister, and downright ancient for they still bought their wives with cowry shells, worth as much as $50 per shell. Weddings were arranged by the fathers of the principals, in sessions of debate and barter that often ascended to high-pitched argument and almost ended in fighting. I don't know whether women's lib has caught up with that part of the world but when we were there native wives did not sleep with their husbands, being banished to snooze with the pigs and other household animals.

There was no evidence of any art form except self-adornment and there were no totems or religious or architectural forms of any distinction. The jungle telegraph consisted of people getting on to high places and yodelling in rising and falling cadences. It must have been practice for mourning at funerals where the prolonged, hideous lamentations of the attendants were enough to drive a white man to the nearest bar.

Suicide was not unknown and self destruction was usually achieved by drowning.

In the jungle villages the males were well armed with axes, machetes, bow and arrows, and spears. They seemed to have no knowledge of stringed musical instruments but used a variety of log drums with ear-shattering effect.

Contact with civilization had enabled almost every native to acquire a personal mirror, something I learned when I began to notice flashes of heliographed light beaming up to me as I flew over the jungle. I thought at first it was signals from someone stranded in the bush, as would be the case in Canada, but soon found it was merely the natives having fun with their mirrors.

Natives provided the bulk of the human cargo that Crowley machines airlifted and I often came back from a trip with my pockets weighted down with silver, thanks to the natives' insistence in paying for and being paid only in silver shillings. They had a deep-seated suspicion of paper money that recent events in the world market seem to suggest were well-founded.

Their patience is marvellous. They would arrive on Monday for a Wednesday flight, then sit or lie quietly around the airfield until it was time to depart. The passengers from the bush villages were liberally smeared with pig grease and as a result had a hard-to-define odor that is almost impossible to forget.

They loaded into my chopper and draped themselves all over me but I never could get used to that pungent smell. It bothered me so much that I always turned the machine so that they would be leaning away from me as I banked and wouldn't be smearing their grease all over my flying clothes. This meant a 270-degree turn to the left to make a right hand turn of 90 degrees, but it was worth it.

Some of my trips took me to the fine vegetable farms in the Markham area, often associated with mission stations like that at Boana, about 25 miles from Lae, where a veteran German Lutheran was in charge of the situation. He had been there for a quarter-century and by a little honest chicanery, for which the Lord must long ago have forgiven him, he had established one of the finest potato farms on the island. This had been achieved by smuggling in some virus-free, high-grade seed potatoes from Germany. It was quite illegal and also quite the best thing he could have done, for careful cultivation of the original strain has made it possible for his farm to produce potatoes of a quality and flavor to put the best from Idaho or Prince Edward Island to shame. I have never tasted any others half as good and I hope that excellent padre's spuds continue to flourish forever, pleasing others as they did me.

The cleric employed local natives on the farm, and as they worked he taught their children in the mission school, where he saw that they were well grounded in the three R's and the gospel according to Martin Luther.

I was temporarily on duty at Popondetta, an inland town about 150 miles southeast of Lae, when a call came in from a mission station pleading for someone to take a dangerously ill native women to hospital. I tried desperately to respond but for four days I was baulked by bad weather despite chance-taking liftoffs into the wind and overcast. Finally I managed to reach the hill station only to find that the woman, allegedly near death from the effects of a childbirth problem, had recovered. No one at the station had bothered to let me know.

Life with Crowley was hard but I didn't mind the work. What did anger me was the inferior maintenance of the machines I was expected to fly. Crowley had only two engineers for the whole fleet and they, with a couple of native assistants, had to look after everything. A pilot flew alone and was expected to radio back for an engineer if one became necessary on an assignment away from base. It was a system with obvious, glaring defects, dangerous and not helped at all by the devil-may-care attitude of the engineers.

My dissatisfaction reached boiling point the day I flew to Rigo where, after putting down on the southwest coast of the island, about 30 miles below Port Moresby, I checked the machine. Close inspection showed that about half of the two dozen screws holding the drag braces to the laminated, steel edged wooden rotors, were loose. I pried under cracked paint and found that many were stripped and would have to be replaced, or new blades substituted.

I alerted Bruce Evans in Lae and he asked me to fly to Port Moresby where it would be easier to make repairs. With some reluctance I agreed to chance it, arranging to follow the winding road between Rigo and Moresby so that I could put down on or near it in case of trouble.

Despite my foreboding I reached Moresby without trouble. There I was joined by the two engineers, who had flown down in a Crowley Apache, a fixed-wing plane, with Inge as a surprise passenger. I noticed at once that there was no sign of new blades but the engineers assured me they could repair the loose screws by setting them in a glue called Aroldite. The proposal didn't appeal to me for I had no confidence in a machine stuck together with glue, no matter how strong the binder.

The more I thought about it the less I liked it and by the time they had returned, and I found they had neglected to examine the screws along the bottom part of the blades, my mind was made up. There was no way, I told them, that I would fly the machine under these circumstances. They were so upset at realizing how they had scamped the repair job they bolted from the room without finishing their lunch.

When they returned Bruce said he was prepared to fly the chopper back to Popondetta while I flew the Apache back to Lae. That suited me. Bruce loaded up with two passengers and moved out. I can't say I was surprised to learn, upon my arrival at Lae, that the civil aviation department had phoned to report receipt of a garbled message suggesting a Crowley machine was down in the Popondetta area.

167

Sure enough, it was good old foolish Bruce. He had barely been able to get off a Mayday signal before crashing into a large field with such force that both skids folded, the main blades flexed and cut off the tail rotor, and the impact seriously injured the back of one of his passengers. Bruce was lucky. He walked away, dazed but largely unhurt, from a crash he had invited by his foolhardiness.

It would appear that he had gone in ignoring the auto rotation procedure that is the normal practice when a helicopter is in a forced landing procedure.

In this emergency the pilot shuts off the engine and lets the chopper go down with the centrifugal clutch disengaged from the main rotor system. This permits the blades to rotate through the force of the air moving through them as the machine descends. The rotor just windmills and with controls at a full, fine pitch. Given a landing spot you can do an auto rotation with about the same safety as a normal landing.

For the sake of a new set of blades Crowley had been forced to spend thousands of pounds reconstructing the machine. It might have been worse. Bruce and his passengers all might have been killed or I might have become the victim of poor maintenance myself except for that lucky decision to inspect the machine at Rigo.

From that point on my relationship with Crowley ran into heavy weather until, in mid-December, he fired me. The culmination of our trouble came on a Sunday when I flew in two mechanics to assemble a tractor on a jungle hillside where a landing strip was being constructed.

I had flown in the disassembled tractor the day before and I knew it would be easy for the mechanics to put it together again in a few hours. While they worked I carried out another assignment, during which I noticed ominous signs of a weather change and a likely storm that might make our return to Lae impossible that day.

Hurrying back to the ridge I found the tractor in one piece and the mechanics ready to leave. They had noticed the angry sky and were as anxious to depart as I was although it was only three o'clock in the afternoon and their official working day ended at six.

168

We flew back to Lae, getting in about four o'clock, congratulating ourselves about escaping the blow. The next morning Crowley called me in and demanded to know why we had quit work ahead of time. I explained the situation but he professed to be unimpressed. "I'm going to fire you," he said. And he did, exactly one week before Christmas.

It is my belief that the real reason for my discharge was my insistence on good maintenance plus the fact that I was his highest-paid employee and, in addition, the most independent worker he had.

It was a distinct relief to leave Crowley, for it seemed at the time to mean an end to chance-taking, such as the time I found myself flying over 52 miles of open sea from Lae to LapLap in a Cessna 205 that, I belatedly discovered, had no flotation equipment. LapLap was one of those lovely tropical islands they sing about in musical comedies but it had to be reached by a water hop offering at almost any time the prospect of one of those nice tropical storms.

A few days later, when Crowley wanted me to take another leap to LapLap I told him flatly "no flotation gear, no go." Experienced pilots dislike flying fixed-wings with wheels over open water. They have a saying that when a land-based machine goes on a water trip "everything goes into automatic rough." I agree. No doubt it is psychological but on those occasions I'll swear you hear bad engine noises that you never notice on land assignments.

In January, 1966, a couple of weeks after Crowley had rejected my services, I started flying with Territorial Airlines, a company with 12 fixed-wing planes, including Cessna 185's, push-pull, motors-forward-and-aft Cessna 136's, and a Beech Baron. The company operator, a five-foot, four-inch ball of fire, was named Buchanan.

Unfortunately, it was the same old maintenance story: two engineers and a far lower standard than I wanted, resulting in things like the Cessna 185 that caught fire on takeoff when the exhaust system broke loose. And, as is with the case with private lines the world over, we flew grossly overloaded. We used to take out the seats for the four official passengers and jam the space with cargo. In others, cargo and passengers were mixed like punch at a Christmas party. Nobody seemed

169

to worry about it but me—not even the civil aviation department blokes.

Working for Territorial took Inge and me to Goroka, a town about 150 miles west of Lae, set in a valley about 5000 feet above sea level. There was a very bad road from Lae to Gorka, so bad we had to send the Volkswagen over it in a lorry. We lived in a one-bedroom apartment, in a row of eight built on the far side of the airfield.

This job was entirely jungle flying to mission airstrips, some of them set on sloping runways along ridges 7,000 or 8,000 feet up. You came in uphill and took off downhill, and be darned to the wind direction. It was a bit hairy at times but you got used to it.

One of the mission stations on the radio circuit to which we were linked had the unusual name of Maprik, one that created howls of laughter around the circuit when the padre reporting the conditions as, "Maprik is wet and slippery."

I guess I flew as much varied freight for Territorial as I ever did anywhere. Sometimes I would have as many as 10 live, 100-pound pigs in the Cessna 180, their feet tied together to prevent them from charging around. They grunted and they defecated and made a horrible scene. I really was worried that one of them might break loose and I carried a revolver at all times on those runs, for a pig, terrorized by the flight, could have wrecked the machine if it broke loose.

At other times I flew out sides of freshly-butchered beef, the carcasses laid out on canvas to keep the blood from soiling the interior of the plane.

It was cooler at Goroka, thanks to the elevation, but it lacked a few other things available in Lae, such as fresh water. At Goroka our water was collected and stored in rainwater tanks. There was no sewage system and one of our neighbors suffered a horrible accident when he fell through the rotted wooden cover of his septic tank.

Somehow I don't think his pride was restored merely because his insurance company paid his claim for a ruined wrist watch.

I got a rare fright one day in a Cessna 336, the push-pull job, while answering a medical alert with a doctor and nurse

170

as passengers. There was a loud explosion in mid-air and all the electrical installations in the instrument panel were knocked out. I concluded that there was a defect in a newly-installed engine and radioed my position, my course and other pertinent data to the nearest station.

Then I sat back and plotted what I would do when the engine coughed to a stop, as I figured it was bound to do soon. It never did. We sailed serenely on without any other startling event. Later mechanics told me the explosion was in a condenser in one of my radio sets. I was still too shaken to be truly grateful for the information.

Territorial had a bit of everything, including the only female pilot in New Guinea. She was an Australian who had been an excellent flying instructor but, unfortunately, had absolutely no bush flying experience. She finally cracked up on an uphill runway on one of those bush strips, which seemed to indicate to management she wasn't quite ready for regular assignments.

A new pilot in that part of the world has to prove his or her right to Captain into the primitive air strips by flying in five times with another pilot familiar with the field. It was a sensible enough precaution but I'm not sure that it was invariably followed up on. The quality of assistance available depended in a large measure on the ability of the companion pilot.

I came away from Goroka with one unusual memento, a quiverful of hand-made native arrows, about two dozen in all, presented to me by some villagers grateful for the services rendered by me and my machine. I have given away most of the arrows to friends but still have a few hung on the walls of my home as visible evidence of some unbelievable years on the other side of the globe.

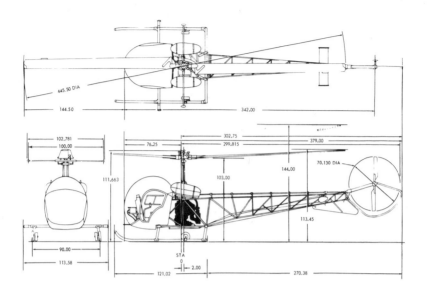

Figure 1-1.  Principal Dimensions - Helicopter

172

# 12
# Flying Shepherd

From the air New Zealand is an undulating green carpet spotted with white mushrooms. It is another Emerald Isle, but the mushrooms, I quickly learned, were some of the vast flocks of sheep that live on this remote, beautiful land. The North Island alone is reputed to have 32 million sheep, more than 10 times the number of people in the whole country. It struck me they ought to have a leg of lamb in at least one quarter of the national flag, sheep are that important to New Zealand's economy.

There was a choice of work there for me in the summer of 1966, for prior to leaving New Guinea I had sent inquiries about employment to five New Zealand firms and received five affirmative replies from which Inge and I had to make a somewhat blind selection since we knew little of any of them.

We finally settled on Helicopters N.Z., and set out for the Maori country via Australia where we stopped over for a couple of weeks in Sydney before flying on to New Zealand. One reason for that visit was the necessity for me to renew my passport. This could be done only at the Canadian consulate in Canberra where, contrary to the doleful predictions of my Australian friends, the business was accomplished with friendly dispatch.

Helicopters N.Z. had its headquarters in the city of Nelson, on the South Island. We traveled there via

Wellington, the national capital, situated on the North Island. Our first impressions were happy ones. On the plane from Australia we got into conversation with an executive in the travel business.

He took charge of us in Wellington, made us feel at home at a cocktail party and helped us set up arrangements for the final leg of our journey. When we arrived in Nelson there was a telegram awaiting us from him welcoming us to our new home and offering best wishes for happiness and success in our life Down Under.

By Canadian standards New Zealand is a small country perhaps a thousand miles in extent from north to south. I doubt if any place is more than 100 miles from the sea. About two-thirds of the population lives on the North Island, which differs markedly from the South where the scene is much more rugged with high, snow-covered mountain peaks.

The green carpet is spread mostly in the north where a landscape of rich beauty is set out in rolling hills, a countryside bathed in sunshine. The weather permits year-round outdoor grazing for the sheep, which are retained in large paddocks, fields that they close crop almost to the grass roots before being moved to another enclosure.

I started flying in New Zealand on my birthday, August 4, my first flip a test flight with John Reid, the chief flying instructor. He checked me out quite thoroughly, making me perform the normal drills including a chopper descent with a dead engine. Then I had to pass a written exam to obtain my New Zealand licence as a commercial pilot. Even then I wasn't quite ready to go to work for I had to take a course in spraying farm areas plagued by gorse and other afflictions.

I had never done any spraying and it was quite a trick to learn to handle a chopper with two 17½-foot booms sticking out, one on each side of the cabin, each with 45 spray nozzles from which 750 pounds of liquid defoliant mixture was ejected.

Gorse was the target of these forays. The yellow-flowered, prickly bush had been introduced into New Zealand by some homesick British settler who wanted to use it as a hedge. Like the rabbits in Australia the imported shrub escaped and ran

174

wild. In certain areas of British Columbia, a similar bush is spreading fast.

In its wild state gorse can grow 12 or 14 feet tall, with spikes a couple of inches long. It can snare an unsheared sheep and is a menace to anyone trying to penetrate it. For control the New Zealanders spray it with a hormone extract, a systemic defoliant similar to the stuff they used on the jungles in Viet Nam. It feeds down to the roots and eventually the plant grows abnormally and then withers up and dies and can be burned off.

It literally grows itself to death, succumbing to giantism.

The gorse flourished in narrow ravines where it was particularly difficult to deal with and from where, if it was left unchecked, it seemed likely to take over the countryside.

John Reid taught me the technique of spraying and for a time we practiced with tanks of plain water until I got the hang of it. Ideally it was a task best done with a forward speed of about 30 miles an hour, with the machine flying 10 or 12 feet above the ground, with the wind at five miles an hour or less.

Properly handled, a chopper carrying 75 gallons of mixture could spray 1½ acres in about 65 seconds, covering the area in 60-foot strips. The solution did not contain any marking coloration so you had to work by memory and pay close attention to the area you were spraying to make sure there was no appreciable area missed.

We sprayed mostly in the morning and towards dusk when the wind was at its lowest point. Wind above five miles an hour would produce dangerous dispersal of the spray that might devastate vegetable and flower gardens and bring on claims for damage to those areas killed by misadventure.

Helicopters N.Z. had eight or nine choppers engaged in spraying, each with ancillary vehicles, including a 2000-gallon water truck tanker and another just to haul the potent spray that was mixed with the water.

My first job was 75 miles away from Nelson working with some forestry people who were engaged in fighting erosion, not gorse. They had to halt erosion on steeper slopes by planting evergreens, no easy job, for the small trees, which came in burlap wrappers with a couple of thousand seedlings

175

rolled up inside them in giant balls, had to be hoisted hundreds of feet from the level plain.

On the steep hills there was no place to put down so I had to unload by hovering as close to the ground as possible and dropping the burlap balls down to the planters who had the devil's own time stopping them from rolling all the way back down the bare, dusty slopes.

Like New Zealanders generally, these planters were ingenious people. The farmers could solve almost any problem as I found when I was assigned to Taumarunui. I was to help in the erection of some fences for sheep paddocks in very rugged country where the task of hauling hundreds of pounds of wire fencing, posts and gates up the hills was a daunting prospect. The sheep farmers had it all figured out. They would lay out on the flat fields the bundles of equipment for the fencing, in just the right order of installation: wire, fence posts, gates and the rest. I picked them up with the helicopter and dropped the material along areas which were marked with flags. Then it was a relatively simple task of sending out the fencing party to pound in the posts and pull the wire tight. It worked marvellously and we could lay several miles of fence in a matter of a few days.

I finally got around to utilizing my spray training at a place called Tekuiti on the North Island. Inge and I were fortunate to find a ready-made home, renting a furnished house from a couple departing to spend a year in Britain. It was rural luxury but it was really too big, with so many extra bedrooms that we found ourselves running a transient hotel for pilots at times. It meant extra work but in a land where frontier hospitality prevails, we followed the local custom to our mutual enjoyment.

It was in Tekuiti I bought a Scotch collie for Inge. He was a beautiful dog, just like Lassie of movie fame. We had a terrible time housebreaking him. I swear he walked around cross-legged until he got in the house.

The spraying business turned out to be a tightly-organized operation controlled by a lively business firm named Dalghety. They had it all pegged. The representatives made an annual swing around the countryside surveying the spraying needs of each farm. They would sell the farmer the spraying service and the hormone that went with it, working out in advance the areas to be treated. A man with 1000 acres might contract to have 200 acres sprayed. It was expensive work for we charged $180 an hour for the helicopter and the hormone cost $300 for a 45-gallon drum, so a buyer of the service didn't spray anything more than his actual needs.

Before starting to spray I went out with the farmer and we examined at close range the areas to be treated. This visit gave me a chance to spot wires that are an eternal menace in this kind of operation. I have never seen a country like New Zealand for wires. They seemed to spring up in the strangest places and they were hard to see and a constant hazard in the low flying operation in which we were engaged.

Some were power lines and doubly dangerous for that reason. Most of them seemed to be telephone lines stretching from farm homes to distant barns and sheep pens. The phone lines bothered me for no matter how much you looked for them you couldn't see them at all. I broke telephone lines on two occasions but fortunately I never got tangled up with a hydro line.

I smashed two lines one day just stooging along looking for a farm on which I was to start a spraying assignment. I couldn't locate it and decided to do the wise thing, ask directions. So I dropped down to a gasoline service station I had spotted along the road. At the very last second I realized there were a couple of wires in the way. It was too late to avoid them, and they were both broken.

The proprietor of the wayside station sauntered out, not a whit disturbed. "Think nothing of it," he said with a smile, as I burbled apologies. "I'll just phone in and tell them to come out and fix it." A second later the light dawned and a funny smile froze on his face. "Christ," he added, "Now I can't phone them, can I?"

My second brush with the pesky wires was somewhat more serious. I was descending to pick up a load of spray mixture from the water truck which was parked near the edge of the road with a steep hill on one side. The hill bothered me for I had to be careful not to have one of the rotor blades strike it and I was being extremely careful with my descent, coming straight in. Just when it all appeared to be ship-shape—

177

wham. I had broken two more telephone wires. I hadn't seen them, and neither had my associates on the spray truck, who were looking right up at them.

This time a piece of broken wire caught around the trim tab of the rotor blades and whirled around until it beat the tail rotor into an unserviceable mess.

That's when I realized that I was in New Zealand, not Canada. It took three days to get spare parts to repair the chopper, quite a contrast to my early experience in the Yukon when we obtained spare parts from Vancouver, some 2000 miles away, in less than a day.

Not that it was hard waiting. The farmers made my life pleasant and seemed unconcerned at the delay. In New Zealand, I discovered, they approach life differently. They seem to believe that a man should be careful to put off until tomorrow almost anything he can do today. It's exasperating to the uninitiated but you get used to it and no one down there seems to get hit by the heart attacks that worry so many of us in North America.

The simple truth is that the New Zealanders seemed to like us, and we certainly liked them. They treated us so well in those country hotels it was unreal. Sometimes I had to get up at two or three o'clock in the morning because I had to drive 40 or 50 miles to be ready to start spraying at first light.

Any time that happened the hotel manager would remind me that the kitchen would be left open so that we could fix ourselves a breakfast and a snack to take away.

On one happy week spent with Inge in a hotel at Matamata the hotel manager was so delighted by our visit that he wouldn't take any payment for our room.

I hardly knew how to thank him but finally settled on inviting him to take a ride in the helicopter. I guess it was as fine a gesture of thanks as I could have devised. He enjoyed every minute of his first helicopter trip which included a run around the neighboring countryside followed by a low level look at the local race track. A gang of men were repairing the grandstand but they all downed tools and watched as I took my genial host around the track at ground level for a couple of circuits. The course was laid out for hurdle racing and we

178

went over each hurdle as it appeared, just like a jumper in a race.

Sometimes I had my work cut out when the spray got into areas where it wasn't wanted. After completing a job on a large sheep ranch I was invited by the owner to join him and his wife for tea. He warned me not to put the chopper down on the magnificent lawn surrounding their home. "We had a fellow in here last year," he explained, "and he came down on the lawn and the residue from the damned machine killed all the grass and ruined the flower beds." I could understand his concern for he had a lovely home, complete with swimming pool and a setting in that beautiful countryside that would be the envy of any city dweller in the world.

Sometimes I even had to be less than frank, such as the occasion we parked the spray truck under some trees overnight. Some weeks later passing that way I stopped and the owner of the property engaged me in conversation during which he asked my opinion about what mysterious blight was affecting the leaves on this small group of trees. I told him I was no expert in the field and couldn't imagine what it could be.

Moving on from Matamata I landed in Teawamutu where Inge and I took quarters in a motel. It was more of that pleasant rural living and the weather was so grand that from time to time Inge came along with me on spraying assignments, a habit that brought her a real scare on one occasion.

She and my loader driver named Tony accompanied me on this particular jaunt. We were working hilly country and I had to land the chopper on an incline. It was some hours before we returned. We'd all climbed in. I started the motor, let the engine warm up and then proceeded to lift off.

To my consternation the chopper began to tilt at a crazy angle and threatened to plunge into the ground. I fought to control it, worried that the rotors would strike the hillside and upset the machine.

Fortunately the hill fell away on the side toward which we were tilting, half-sliding with the rotors spinning erratically. I was beginning to get the machine under control when the starboard spray boom smacked into a large gorse bush, the impact driving the boom back against the side of the

179

helicopter at a 90-degree angle to its normal position. Fortunately, it did not strike the tail rotor.

We managed to avoid crashing and gradually the machine righted itself and I was able to fly it down to a level spot where I put it down and examined the damage. I tied the damage spray boom securely to the tail boom but could find no other damage.

Then I figured out what had happened. The chopper was equipped with two tanks, one on each side of the cabin, with a crossfeed connection. While the machine was parked on the slope the fuel from the upper tank had run down and completely filled the tank on the low side. It happened to be on the side where my passengers were situated, an arrangement that so shifted the center of gravity that it had been almost impossible to fly the machine. I ought to have realized that the fuel would have altered its normal position but in the euphoria of that day in the country I didn't. I had been a bit too blase. Once more I was sharply reminded that familiarity, while it may not breed contempt, can sure become the father of a whole lot of carelessness.

Although there was much that was enjoyable, my employment with the spraying firm presented ever-present dangers because of the geography of the work areas. My worst experience came shortly after the hillside scare. My chopper, struggling to get up with a full load of spray, 75 gallons weighing 750 pounds, was caught in a strong downdraft and refused to respond to the controls as it was sucked down.

I tried to dump the load of spray but neither the automatic electric release or the hand release would respond. I went down, down, down, before the eyes of my horrified associates at the spray truck from which I had lifted off only a couple of minutes before.

An added consideration in my fight to avoid disaster was my awareness that a heavy steel cable was stretched across the area and that if I hit it in my almost-out-of-control condition I might be in real trouble.

I spotted a small, bare, level patch and did my best to head for it as the ground came up remorselessly to claim me. About 20 feet above the ground I shut off the engine, to avoid the danger of fire, and felt that while I would have a rough landing it would be a relatively safe one.

At that juncture the main rotor blades collided with a large punkah tree, about 16 inches in diameter. The collision flipped the machine over on its side and we went in with a crash that knocked me unconscious. The rotors as they ground to a halt, came close to battering the machine to bits, destroying the tail assembly in their wild gyrations. I must have been unconsious for several minutes, long enough for my companions, who were 600 yards or more down the road, to run up to the top of the bank below which I had come to disaster.

The machine was separated from the bank, which was the shoulder of a road, by a small stream. I released my harness and fell from the chopper, still half dazed, my one intention to get away from it before it exploded or burned. I found a fallen log over the stream and climbed across on this unexpected natural bridge. When I got to the other side I found I was clutching a shattered thermos bottle, something that totally astonished me. I threw it as far away as I could and was helped up to the road level.

By that time a car, occupied by a man and a middle-aged woman who turned out to be a nurse, had drawn up.

The woman seemed more shocked by my appearance than I had been by the accident and kept apologizing because she had no first aid materials to help me. "I've only got a couple of aspirins," she kept explaining. To calm her down I painfully swallowed them, and she seemed satisfied she had done her best.

The machine was badly damaged, although not a writeoff. I could only assess the mishap in retrospect and thank my lucky stars I had had the foresight to cut the engine. There is nothing that bothers a pilot more than the danger of fire in a crash.

For a brief period I worked with another firm based at Haast, on the west coast of the South Island near Mount Cook, a job that took me into one of the most unusual assignments of my 30 years in flying.

New Zealand has no predators and wild animals are more likely to die of old age than anything else. As a result the deer population of the islands tends to explode and there was at that time a large population of them in the Mount Cook area and someone in government decided it must be reduced.

These deer were an environmental menace for they were so numerous that they sometimes grazed the countryside down to the grass roots on the slopes, causing erosion conditions with the heavy rainfall of the area.

The animals ranged in highly inaccessible places, far too difficult to reach and too remote to attract the ordinary sportsman hunter who might have helped control their numbers, so the authorities turned to professional hunters to help thin out the herds, with the use of helicopters to lift them to the rough places in which the deer would be found. We took the door off the right side of the choppers and moved in two-man teams of exterminators, armed with semi-automatic rifles to knock over the deer from the air with a minimum of discomfort. It really was very much like that Christmas hunt with the Crees in Manitoba.

The team consisted of a hunter and a gutter. I would fly them around the mountains until we spotted a herd. Frequently we located them in a narrow ravine, perhaps as many as 40 deer at a time. Once we had them in sight I kept circling or hovering in mid-air until my Deadeye Dick passenger had shot them down. Then I would descend and let off the gutter who would slit their throats and remove their intestines and get the carcasses ready to be lifted out. While he worked I would take the shooter away to locate and knock over another herd. It was a terrible job, the worst I have ever had, and I hated every minute of it.

Returning to the killing ground I would find the deer dressed and stacked ready for me to lift off a dozen at a time. I flew them to some level assembly ground where a Cessna 180 would land and fly them off to our camp some 60 miles away. five helicopters averaged about 100 deer each per day.

When there was a big enough load, refrigerated trucks would transport the venison to Christchurch for processing and then onto refrigerated ships that took the meat to a ready market in Europe. They tell me venison is a delightful main course when properly cooked.

It was hard, dangerous work with real perils for the

182

chopper pilot because there was an ever-present possibility that the swaying load of carcasses, lifted on a short chain, would knock into the side of a hill.

The slopes were such that you could not find a level spot and had to hover while the venison was attached to the hook.

Several helicopters were written off when their rotor blades hit the hills when the machines were caught in gusts of wind, but the worst accident happened to a party of hunters and threw a pall of gloom over the whole operation.

It was one of those unbelievable things. The pilot had put the helicopter down on a small level area beside a steep hillside and both the hunting team members had climbed out. They shot a deer at once, behind the small hill, and reappeared higher up the slope dragging the carcass down toward the chopper.

They were walking backwards, tugging at the deer, so intent on moving it that they forgot the whirling rotors of the machine whose engine was running. The pilot sat frozen in the cab shouting warnings that the two men could not hear as they backed into the rotors. Both were instantly beheaded.

The impact damaged the blades, making it impossible for the pilot to fly the machine. He was forced to hike out 18 miles through rough country with his bizarre story of tragedy in the mountains.

Of all my experiences this was the most dangerous and traumatic and I was glad when they called off the assignment although it had been a most lucrative one, bringing in as much as $3000 a month.

With the global demand for lamb at a low ebb, and wool prices down, things were not good in New Zealand and Inge and I were undecided whether to remain or return to Canada. Our immediate future was settled when a widow, owner of a 750-acre sheep farm near Taumarunui, persuaded us to move in and help her run the establishment. We had been living up to the very good income I had been earning and, like most pilots, I suspect, had no great resources on which to fall back so we welcomed this opportunity to work with Dawn Agnew, a middle-aged, kindly employer who became our very good friend.

She took quite a chance at that for neither of us knew

anything about conventional farming, and even less about a New Zealand sheep farm.

In fact we found it enjoyable. I think I did everything there was to be done. Both of us learned to ride horseback, and operate tractors. I built fences, and did all the many jobs required on a farm. Dawn had some 2000 ewes and 100 rams and at lambing time the place was a pandemonium for almost every one of the ewes had twins and suddenly there were 6000 sheep around.

She also owned two bulls and 100 head of cattle, and four of the smartest sheep dogs you ever saw. Those dogs astonished us, the way they took charge of the sheep, who must be among the most stupid of four-footed creatures.

One day Inge and I were given the job of shepherding some 600 sheep to a new paddock. We rode horses and trying to get those sheep to move off in the right direction was the wildest thing you ever saw. They swarmed all over the place, heading in every direction but the way we wanted them to move, an uncontrollable mass of bleating wool.

Dawn sat on her horse on a hill overlooking the scene and I guess she must have laughed herself silly. Finally she took pity on us and rode down to help us with the four dogs. Inside of a couple of minutes those dogs had taken command and had the sheep in marching order. It was unreal, just beautiful to watch.

I admired those dogs but I had a healthy respect for the bulls who had a mean way of looking at you over their shoulder. One day at the beginning of our stay on the farm I had to walk through a field in which they were pastured, a sortie that bothered me more than somewhat. I suggested that I ought to take along a shotgun in case I came across some of the wild turkeys that lived on the property. I moved warily along, gun at the ready. The bulls belched a couple of times, looked at me once and turned away. I'll swear they were laughing.

We used to shoot wild pigs as well as turkeys and let me tell you there is no gourmet dish to surpass properly prepared and roasted wild pig. The meat flavor is fantastically good and soon makes you forget how ugly the animals looked, black and spotted, running around the woods.

Shearing is a communal occasion on a sheep farm. All the neighbors come around to help, starting work about five o'clock in the morning. They knock off for breakfast about eight, appetites at the ready for the masses of food prepared for them, lamb chops, platters of fried eggs, mounds of potatoes, bread, butter, the whole thing, and how those sheep men can eat.

I watched with wonder, my stomach simply not up to the task presented.

I learned quickly but I had to go from a standing start and must have been one of the greenest hands Dawn had ever seen. One day she sent me along with some bales of hay to feed some cattle in a distant field. I tossed the bales over the fence and left it at that. It wasn't until the next day that I learned you were supposed to open the bales, remove the string and spread the fodder around.

We enjoyed seven months on the farm but finally decided that we didn't want to make it our life's work. With great reluctance we announced our decision to return home, much to the sorrow of our good friend Dawn who pleaded with us to stay.

New Zealand was one of the happiest chapters of our life abroad but we were overjoyed to get back to Canada in March, 1968, full of experiences that made us understand that there really is no place like home.

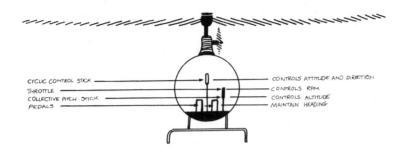

CYCLIC CONTROL STICK ——————————— CONTROLS ATTITUDE AND DIRECTION

THROTTLE ——————————— CONTROLS RPM

COLLECTIVE PITCH STICK ——————————— CONTROLS ALTITUDE

PEDALS ——————————— MAINTAIN HEADING

186

# 13
# Homecoming

When I returned to Canada in mid-1968 I took a job with Northward Aviation of Edmonton flying fixed-wings— Beech 18 and Otters with both wheels and floats. Helicopter jobs were scarce at the time and I rather looked forward to the conventional machines because fixed wing pilots usually got back to civilization at night, which would be a nice change from living in a tent in the bush in some God-forsaken spot.

In truth, it wasn't all that cushy flying the conventionals. On floats you had to descend on the lakes and rivers, usually to tie up at the rudest kind of docks. Because the machines had no reversible pitch props it was a bit dicey docking at one of the impromptu docks, for you had to swing the machine in a split-second shift of course to bring it alongside the dock and permit it to be tied up. Rarely was anyone there to handle the rope so I usually found myself leaping from the cabin onto the slippery floats and reaching wildly for something to which I could tie up the plane in my secondary role as docking attendant. It demanded a high degree of timing and agility and had other hazards that I discovered when my glasses fell from my shirt pocket into 30 feet of water and I couldn't recover them. The loss didn't mean I would literally be flying blind but it did embarrass me in map reading, which was difficult for me without them.

My joyfully anticipated return to the conventionals turned out to be a dismal experience all round for I found I was to be stevedore as well, responsible for loading and unloading up to 1500 pounds of cargo per flight. After three months I abandoned this as not what I desired, for the truth is that such flying demands a two-man crew that some airlines are just too niggardly to provide.

One of my assignments was an unusual one. I was pilot of one plane of two used to take Prime Minister Trudeau on a trip to the Arctic regions, to places like Tuktyuktuk and others in that general area. The Prime Minister's party was accompanied by an R.C.M.P. inspector in charge of security, the arrangements for which failed to impress me at all. I was so unimpressed, in fact, that I mentioned it to the inspector who was sitting in a seat beside me. "How do you know I don't have a gun?" I asked him. He looked surprised. Warming to my subject, I continued. "This is ridiculous. There is absolutely no security check. Here we are, thousands of feet up in the air. Suppose I'm out to get you or someone is out to get the Prime Minister."

The total lack of curiosity by the so-called security forces left me baffled. One 'nut' in the right place at the right time could have written the story of the year without the guards being able to do anything about it.

After Northward, relieved and grateful, I went back to flying choppers with Shirley Helicopters of Edmonton. They wanted me in a hurry but I didn't find out why until later. I was sent at once in a helicopter to a camp at the junction of the MacKenzie and Okra rivers where I was to tell the resident pilot to fly his chopper out to Hay River for a routine inspection. Later I discovered that the company wanted to fire the pilot but only after he had moved his machine to a point where it could easily be recovered. I was told he was a bit of an aerial 'cowboy' with a taste for flying under bridges and things like that which had resulted in one writeoff crash.

The Okra River camp's remoteness was one feature we found a bit hard to take, so visitors were welcome and eagerly awaited. One day as I flew back to camp I spotted a boat on the Mackenzie with a number of people on board. I

188

waved to them, pointing to our camp, and made motions that I was descending and would like them to follow.

Obviously they didn't understand, for we were disappointed to see they were docking on the other side of the river, which is a couple of miles wide at that point. A little later I saw heavy black rain clouds heading our way. They usually heralded a downpour and I realized our distant visitors might be drenched. I flew over and invited them to join us, something they very quickly did. We helped them put up their tents and all of us were nicely started into dinner when the storm struck.

It rained for four straight days and nights during which we became good friends with the visiting family, a Calgary lawyer and his wife, daughter and son. He had a proper, custom-built, 35-foot river boat with twin outboards and a tentlike structure in the middle of it. They had started at Fort Nelson and were on their way down river to Inuvik. We enjoyed their company and appreciated the way they mucked in to help run the camp. The hospitality of the frontier is a very real thing and all of us benefitted from the tradition.

Okra was a good camp but since such camps are not permanent the dwellers have to put up with some primitive things such as temporary, outdoor privies.

Ours at Okra was some distance from the camp but many feet had cleared and worn a reasonably smooth path to the establishment to which all must resort at some time or other.

On one occasion an associate excused himself and headed down the trail. No one thought anything about it until, much later and long after he should have returned, his absence was made evident by distant shouts for help, that sounded tinged with panic.

A rescue party dashed off down the trail and determined that the cries were coming from the biffy. The reason for the distress was a large black bear, seated in the middle of the path, regarding the rickety structure with a curious eye.

The inmate had been sitting there meditating when the bear strolled up, took one look and sat down. The biffy occupant kept silent for a time, perhaps in the traditional belief that if you don't move a bear won't bother you. But after a time he began to get worried and started to shout. The more he shouted the more disturbed he became, and the less the bear seemed to care.

Bruin finally beat a slow retreat when the reinforcements arrived. There may be a moral in this story but I'm not sure what it can be, unless it is that biffy users on the Okra ought to carry firearms.

I stayed with Shirley Helicopters through 1969 working mostly with geologists and prospectors in the Norman Wells and Yellowknife areas. One of my customers was an aging prospector, possibly in his seventies, who wanted to take a look at some property and was very insistent about travel arrangements.

As we scooted along the shores of Great Slave Lake he told me why. Pointing down to a small island several miles from shore, he said that he had spent a week on it a few years before. It was an experience he wasn't likely to forget. He had been put down on the island by a fixed-wing plane which had agreed to pick him up the next day. He had a blanket, a small axe, a package of sandwiches and a few matches.

But the plane didn't show the following morning, or the day after that, or the day after that. A week went by, and the stranded passenger was getting somewhat cranky from camping out with a minimum of necessities, before the plane showed up.

He might have been there for the rest of his life if his wife hadn't telephoned the airline in Yellowknife from Vancouver to ask if they knew anything about her husband who hadn't arrived home when expected.

Horrified company officials had to confess they had forgotten all about him, and hurried to redress an oversight that was downright embarrassing to them and distressing to the customer. I can only hope they refunded his charter fees.

It's a scary area in which to work. There are no landmarks but the lakes, and there are thousands of them, large and small. Your compass can be 100 degrees off north because of magnetic distortion and if you aren't a good navigator you can be in real trouble.

In May, 1970, I went to work with Lift Air International, under the direction of my very dear friend, Neil Armstrong, who had been my boss with Sparton during the seal hunt days. They had a contract with the B.C. government to do a topographical survey in northern B.C. Crews of men with instruments to triangulate measurements were involved. They worked on the peaks of mountains, some of them up to 11,000 feet high.

Sometimes there was no place to land on the peak and I had to drop them as close to it as I could. We started out at Dease Lake, worked over to Rainbow Lake and generally enjoyed an elevated life that made the use of supercharged choppers a comfort as well as a necessity.

The winds at times made life dangerous. I was flying in gales up to 45 miles an hour, which makes it a high-risk operation. After a couple of months I was assigned to a team near Norman Wells that was cutting seismic lines to the east of that community. I was on call 18 hours a day, from 6 a.m. until midnight. It was a busy year. In the last days of July I was helping fight a monstrous forest fire in Wood Buffalo National Park, working with the forestry people. They had six helicopters, a dozen bulldozers, fixed-wing water bombers, and hundreds of men to fight the fire which was almost dead center between Hay River and Fort Smith.

I finished up the year working with a survey party lining up the route for the proposed MacKenzie Valley pipeline. They had large hand augers and were doing test drilling to check the depth of the perma frost all the way up to the Yukon border from Rainbow Lake 90 miles west of High level.

My flying was limited in 1971, restricted pretty much to a brief spell with a fishing lodge on Great Bear Lake. This American-owned and operated resort could accommodate about 45 guests, who paid $100 a day for the privilege of fishing for the huge lake trout inhabiting the waters.

Every weekend the lodge operator hired a DC-6 from Pacific Western Airlines in Edmonton which would fly in the new batch of fishermen and take out the departing guests. It was a really hairy operation, for the charter pilot had to put the four-motor plane down on a short, narrow, sandy runway at Sawmill Bay, some 850 miles north of Edmonton. It was fringed by small trees and when the plane halted its wings would reach out over the closest of them. From there the fishermen were lifted to the lodge in three smaller float planes.

Early in 1972 I joined Don Crowe of Nahanni Helicopters for what looked likely to be a busy and exciting year. To begin with I had to familiarize myself with flying S-55 converted turbine Sikorsky helicopters, 11-passenger machines with a 3500-pound payload. The assignment took us to Richards Island, about 90 miles north of Inuvik on the 69th degree latitude north, 200 miles above the Arctic circle, where teams from Gulf Oil were doing seismic test drilling.

It is low, slightly rolling country, with no eminences of any consequence on the landscape, barren and snow-covered when we began work in March.

The conditions were the most dangerous I have ever experienced for we worked a good deal of the time in a white fog, sometimes flying 10 or 12 feet above the ground with a forward visibility of about 100 years.

Usually we followed tractor trails on the snow and ice to get back to the camp.

After Richards Island we moved down to another camp some 280 miles below Inuvik where I served two groups of prospectors. Things had changed in the north since my first experiences and there had developed an obvious concern for the environment that I had not seen before.

For example it was now forbidden to leave empty fuel drums on the camp area. They had to be airlifted out, along with all other disposable refuse. Not even a tin can could be left behind.

This program will delight environmentalists as much as it distressed exploration firms' treasurers as they tote up the extra cost of the cleanup. The helicopter I was flying rented at $350 an hour, not including the cost of fuel, oil, and the pilot's wages.

Those same environmentalists will also be pleased to know that federal officials keep a close watch on camp sites and sternly insist that the new regulations be obeyed.

It was hard, interesting work, but when, at the end of April, I flew back to Inuvik at ground level with visibility ahead about 400 yards, I was flying out of this special, precious world of aviation. A few weeks later my heart grounded me and I learned that my future association with the industry would be, at best, flying a desk somewhere in the great world of air travel.

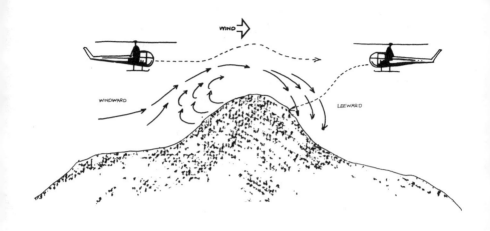

# 14

# Make Mine Flying

If I were, once more, a young man searching for a career, would I become a flyer today? People often ask me that and I think about it from time to time. Invariably the answer comes out a solid "YES".

In a world where many complain of the hum-drum, the deadly dullness of their life and chosen vocation, the flyer moves in a very demanding, highly exciting and generally rewarding calling—and I don't mean just financially. It is a way of life, one in which the sky is the limit and where the future may beckon even to the remoter regions of space. They are going to need pilots for those re-usable space shuttles.

The flyer has the satisfaction of becoming a genuine professional, with an opportunity to perform usefully for the good of all.

Once his craft leaves the ground he is the arbiter of his destiny and of all those who fly with him. He is in complete command as are the captains of sea-going ships who have for centuries defied the perils of the deep.

There is no easy way to become a flyer. Pilots are made, not born. Coming to instruction with mental and physical qualities to meet the continuing challenge of the vocation is a good start but resolution and perseverance and the willingness to strive for perfection are also necessary.

195

You can't get your pilot's wings by studying books alone, although you won't win them without study. It takes years of training and experience and the steady advance in technology ensures that you never stop learning no matter how many flying hours you may have logged.

Perhaps I'm prejudiced but I'm convinced that the best route to a pilot's wings and the skills of an accomplished airman—the place where novices can learn with the best instructors and the best equipment—leads through the air force. Today they call it the air component of the armed forces but that is window dressing to justify what was quaintly called unification, a political end but hardly a military one.

Like thousands of former Royal Canadian Air Force veterans I have been delighted by recent announcements that the flying service is being reconstituted as a separate arm, and I hope that in due course changing opinions will lead to full restoration of the name of this honorable service and all its magnificent traditions.

In contrast the do-it-yourself way of learning to fly through civilian flying schools is a poor alternative. It is almost certain to be a haphazard approach with a limited variety of aircraft on which to learn, light machines easy to fly but offering little for individuals intent on moving into the direction of the big jets of modern transportation.

In service flying the weeding out of less likely candidates is tough, even ruthless, which is the way it should be.

The truth is that many civilian instructors are not sufficiently demanding. After all, the student is paying substantial fees for his lessons, and all too often the instructor feels he has to give a little. It isn't up to the instructor to pass a student. That ultimate test is conducted by the D.O.T. inspector, who has a minimum standard to follow laid down by the Department of Transport. But it lacks the severity of testing insisted on in the armed forces and I doubt if it will ever approach the service rating in that regard.

For the student learning to fly by private instruction there is the problem of high cost for lessons and even more difficult financial barriers for those keen to advance to handling more sophisticated machines. To achieve a commercial career the student must get through a multi-engine flying course and obtain an instrument rating that will skyrocket the cost of learning into the thousands of dollars.

I'm not saying that someone with brains and desire can't become a good pilot by this route. I do insist that is the most difficult, expensive and least satisfactory way to proceed.

The public attitude to flying has altered beyond recognition in the course of my own career and many expert predictions of where the flying world might be going have been disproven.

We used to hear prophecies that a family air flivver would occupy the garage that once housed the finest products of the automobile industry. Now, although there are thousands of light aircraft on this continent, we understand that this will never happen and vaguely comprehend that it may even be a very good thing the soothsayers blew that one.

More people are flying all the time but they are seated in comfort on commercial airlines, more and more often in flying theatre-restaurants carrying 400 passengers at a time.

There are as many as 110,000 small boats along the western coastline of Canada, but only a few hundred small airplanes. The air vehicle, I suspect, will not advance much beyond that ratio to the pleasure boat.

Aircraft cost too much, are too difficult to handle, and too expensive to maintain to be much more than the toys of the well-to-do and the necessity of larger businesses.

It is difficult to assess the comparative future of the helicopter and conventional aircraft for they are not rivals and in use are more complementary than opposed for they are designed for different types of service. The fact that both fly through the air is the major similarity and it just about ends there.

The fixed wing aircraft is designed to carry heavy loads over long distances utilizing the growing mass of navigational aids and facilities in the plane and at the airports.

The helicopter is designed to haul smaller loads and can operate from much less sophisticated sites.

Versatility is the trademark of the helicopter that permits it to exercise such diverse roles as traffic control on super

197

highways and the capping of tall buildings such as the CN Tower in Toronto.

The chopper pilot has far fewer flying aids and has to function in large measure on sound judgment developed through experience, back-stopped by a sort of sixth sense in which the laws of probability and possibility mingle.

For me, and those like me, the helicopter is a demanding machine but it is fun to fly. So, if I had another choice to make between fixed wing and choppers, I'd waste no time opting for the latter.

One reason, I'm sure, is because I see a continually expanding field of action for the helicopter captain. Copters only came into commercial use in Canada in the second half of the 40s when Okanagan Helicopters started their operations in the interior of British Columbia.

Their first machine was a B model, small open-cockpit machine on wheels, with miniscule lifting capacity. By the time I joined Okanagan in 1957 they were using the Bell 47-G, an immense improvement but a very crude machine compared to helicopters of today and the Sikorsky S-55 and S-58's.

The controls were manually-operated as I have explained. Today's choppers have a hydraulic-assisted system similar to power steering in a car. Engine horsepower has been immensely increased over the 160 HP of the Gs. The last helicopter I flew was a jet-engined Sikorsky S-55, rated at 850 HP but derated to 650 for normal use. The S-55, as a result has 200 HP in reserve for emergency use, somewhat more than the 47-Gs could produce at top performance.

The Bell had a normally aspirated engine which meant that it performed best at ground level and less effectively as height increased. A supercharged engine, on the other hand, maintains ground level power up to 9,000 feet.

This is a great advantage to the pilot who finds loss of power combined with loss of rotor blade effectiveness at higher altitudes because of the thinness of the air. The jet engine overcomes much of this although there is no way the loss of performance of the flexible rotors can be altered and the higher you go the sloppier the chopper becomes in performance.

198

When I first started to fly choppers we cruised at about 45 to 55 miles per hour loaded. The S-55 cruised at 100 mph.

However, military machines used in Vietnam and elsewhere have been fitted to fly around 200 mph using a stiff, non-flexing rotor blade that permits the pilot to do complete loops and rolls. The same sort of stunting with a commercial machine would result in the rotors flexing and destroying the tail assembly.

In a quarter-century the all-round performance of helicopters, their design and capabilities, have advanced immensely. Giant helicopters today can lift up to 10 tons, nearly 20 times the capacity of the 47-Gs.

The added speed is attractive to potential users and horsepower in reserve extends the safety factors.

While piloting my Sikorsky I had occasion to test that power reservoir. One winter's day in the high Arctic I was faced with the problem of having to lift out 14 men to camp before night closed in. The safe way would have been to lift eight or nine and return. But the light was fading and it was certain to me that the remainder would have to face the perils of deadly Arctic cold without protection with real possibility of death from exposure.

It was a gamble with a 50 per cent overload but I quietly patted the big engine, crossed my fingers, and loaded all 14. We took off without a sign of strain. Oh, those lovely extra 200 wild horses! The ordinary helicopter would have lifted for a moment, then sunk slowly back to earth.

I have explained that helicopters all too often are loaded beyond normal capacity, and load limits exceeding specifications become the norm. Pilots get used to it. They load it all, then try a lift. If the machine won't rise they offload until it will. It gives the customer the maximum for his charter dollar but it leaves the pilot without insurance for an emergency. I never knew whether to cheer our nerve or deride our stupidity.

The versatility of the whirlybird never ceases to amaze me. Think of the helicopter in the forests, helping to plant trees, moving men and seedlings to untrodden regions. Otherwise inaccessible woodlots can be reached for cutting and planting and other forestry routines.

In some cases the logging industry utilizes helicopters to lift out selected prime trees, eliminating the need to build expensive logging roads with the environmentally undesirable results that frequently follow road construction. Clean sweep cutting, of course, is something else and choppers are too expensive to move the large quantities of timber in that form of harvesting.

Machines that can lift up to 10 tons come high—as much as $4000 an hour, and their utilization must be carefully planned so that no time is lost when they are working.

In the resource field the role of the helicopter has become vital in the installation and maintenance of pipelines, power transmission lines and in many other ways. Choppers convey workmen, tools and material to sites where power transmission towers will be erected. They move the power lines from one tower to another, placing those wire strings that light homes.

They are ideal for low-level line inspection. I have flown an 800-mile inspection on a pipeline from Fort St. John to Vancouver. The chopper can get right down low into the valleys for a close look at problems, such as washouts or slides, that can rupture lines and permit oil or gas to escape. Fixed wing planes simply are unable to handle this sort of inspection.

In New Zealand, as I have related, choppers helped sheep herders place fences on hill tops, sprayed crops and even lifted out official kills of deer from mountain nooks and crannies.

Their role in fighting forest fires becomes more important as their lifting capability increases. Helicopters can fill water buckets at small sloughs and at ponds close to the fire scene, where conventional water bombers may have to fly many miles to find a lake large enough to provide them with takeoff and landing room.

Helicopters frequently rescue endangered people on stricken vessels that could not be reached in time by other ships. Their role in air-sea rescue is so important that I am among the many who wonder why the Canadian government cannot accede to pleas for a dramatic expansion of this service on both our East and West coasts. Recent events have once more demonstrated that at the south end of Vancouver Island the safety of Canadian vessels in trouble and the people aboard them can only be served by U.S. Coast Guard equipment and personnel because the single air-sea rescue base is at Comox, 150 miles away.

Saving lives, in fact, is one of the most significant roles of the helicopter. The helicopter can detect downed airplanes and vessels in distress, can retrieve the injured and put them down in stretchers on the front lawns of the nearest hospitals. Additionally, this versatile and exciting machine has developed from the life-saving role of aerial ambulance in war to an armored strike craft capable of carrying troops,

The more I read and hear about the desirability of using short-takeoff-and-landing aircraft (STOL) to provide a service from the center of one urban area to another the more I wonder why no one has seriously looked at a major helicopter service.

Today's helicopters can lift the equivalent of 115 people. They can average close to 200 miles an hour. Why not a Toronto-Ottawa-Montreal helicopter service? Or a regular schedule from Vancouver to Seattle, Portland and San Francisco?

All that is needed is the development of improved cabin design to provide proper passenger accommodation. The helicopter, I submit, is the answer to flying from one city center to another, not the STOL. Large helicopters haul passengers from New York and other large metropolitan area airports to skyscraper heliports so the problems of operating in a big city have been resolved in advance.

There is no doubt that governments will continue to expand their air-sea rescue and patrol services. With 200-mile fishing limits the nations of the world are almost certain to develop mother ships for helicopter fleets that will maintain those sea rights. Airplanes can do the high level spotting but only helicopters can descend to the sea level for the close look that is going to be required.

For the young man who isn't attracted by an assembly line, or a career behind an office desk or a bank counter, flying those helicopter patrols of the future might be a much more rewarding occupation. And for men of my age there may even be the feeling that we were born 30 years too soon, for the golden age of the helicopter is only dawning.

When I look at the job of flying a helicopter I keep hoping that as this expansion comes it will be accompanied by a more intense and sophisticated look at the potential helicopter captain.

I say this because flying a helicopter demands special talents above and beyond those needed to pilot a conventional plane. The chopper pilot must have an unusual degree of co-ordination. His reflexes should be unusually good. The pilot of a commercial aircraft has a sizeable crew to spell him off. The helicopter pilot works pretty much on his own.

There are numerous cases of excellent fixed wing pilots who have been unable to make the transition to whirlybirds.

It would be a comfort to me, on the sidelines, to feel that stricter testing will be required by an improved breed of Transport Department examiners, although I somehow doubt that this will happen.

For my part I have some substantial reservations about the quality of some government test pilots who examine candidates for licences to fly helicopters. The reason I wonder about the quality of government testing is that the civil servant helicopter test pilot is paid about one-third as much as a good pilot with a private firm.

I suspect that the brightest, most highly-motivated and competent pilots are unlikely to be attracted to government service because of that huge differential in reward. And I believe that test pilots should be among the best in the business to ensure that only the most properly qualified candidates become pilots.

This criticism may well be unfair to some but it will certainly be true of others and it needs to be said. Flying is not a right but a privilege beyond the dreams of most men and women.

Still, one thing to remember is that you don't have to have some special type of mechanical mind to learn to fly. A knowledge of engines can be helpful, and a course to enable you to understand what they do for you and to establish the respect that should be accorded them, certainly is most

202

desirable, if only to make sure you don't overstress the engine and mess it up. You need to have some technical knowledge of the structure of the craft, too, so that you avoid asking it to perform feats beyond the limits for which it was designed.

I have never been called upon to make any major repairs to an aircraft. That is the job of the specialist engineer and the pilot should leave it to him, perhaps in view of the changing times I should say him or her, in all my references to flying. There are pilot engineers on aircraft, licenced for both roles, but generally they are engineers who have learned to fly after acquiring their other skills, and they are relatively few in number. My own feeling is that no man can do a double job well through a full day. Either his mechanical duties suffer or he will not be as good a pilot as he ought to be. They are different, difficult and tiring tasks, best kept separate.

Throughout my story I have, from time to time, made a number of criticisms of flying safety. I ought to put it in focus. Generally, flying standards are among the best and safest of any in any area of human activity when they are applied properly. All the necessary rules and regulations are there to ensure good maintenance, for example, but you will know by now that they are often ignored, or not followed to the degree that prudence and common sense would suggest. I'm speaking now of the small operator, not the major airlines, especially those in Canada, such as Air Canada and C.P. Air which have the finest safety records in the world. They don't try to cut corners to save a dollar for they know it is foolhardy to skimp where the default may bring about a major accident that could cost millions.

Some of the owners of small private lines have no such inhibitions, as I think I have demonstrated. And it can cost them, as it did that firm in New Guinea which substituted glue for new parts in the chopper rotor blades and paid for it with a crash that cost thousands of dollars for repairs and placed at hazard the lives of three people.

Like all the other rules man designs, the air traffic regulations are only as good as the people applying them. I would say that 98 per cent of air accidents arise from human

203

error and only rarely do machines go down from technical failures. Aircraft are designed and constructed to withstand all of the stresses and situations that will arise in normal flight, and many components far beyond normal stresses. When you read of an aircraft crashing into a height of land while making an approach to landing it is almost certain that this was not the fault of instruments but the result of human error.

It is one of the inescapable facts of flying that the moment of greatest peril to the craft comes during a landing, at a time when the crew may be tired from hours of flying duty. There is tremendous pressure on the pilot at most times, but he has to overcome the worst of it at the time he is least fitted to do so.

In bush flying the pilot simply does not have sufficient aides from the ground, such as radio and navigational help. The cost of upgrading the few installations in Canada's vast northern expanses to normal standards would be prohibitive. Helicopters can never expect quite the same standard of assistance as conventionals for they frequently do not fly to fixed points and no one can know where to establish communications systems that could best serve them.

The greatest, and much more subtle, pressure on bush pilots is imposed by owners who insist on overloading, and who work their pilots and crew through every available minute of the day, regardless of the fatigue buildup accentuated in the pilot. There is an urgency to do the job as cheaply and as quickly as possible, in order to enhance the profit picture. The pilot usually is well paid but always lurking in his mind is the fear that if he insists on operating by the regulations he will find himself jobless, supplanted by a more compliant replacement.

Working with small airlines I had no scheduled days off. You went up every day, Christmas or New Year's, the same as any other, as long as the sky looked favorable. In this situation you rest only when the weather closes in, and in all my 16 years of helicopter jockeying I can't think of any more than two or three days when I arbitrarily decided I needed a rest and did not fly despite the weather's verdict that I could.

All my experience points to the truth of the common

expression among chopper pilots, to which I have already made reference, that there are two kinds of pilots: those who have had an accident and those who are about to.

Many of the pilot's problems are the fault of the money-hungry souls — I've worked for a few — who skimp on maintenance and set up impossible working schedules. They look at it with unbelievable callousness. As long as a craft will fly they're satisfied. If it crashes, with any luck the insurance will cover it. And if the crew is victim of the accident, well, flyers can always be replaced. These are the outfits that need much closer scrutiny than they get in remote places of the world, a condition that means they flourish because governmental officials responsible for aircraft rule enforcement are not doing their jobs. They appear blind to the most obvious cases of neglect, and I speak of conditions in many parts of the world, not just in Canada.

After 30 years of life in a job I loved, my own career came to a grinding halt four years ago after a totally unexpected heart attack. I had no advance warning. There were no signals of what was to come, no pain, no shortness of breath, nothing. Even when it happened it was so far from my mind that I found it difficult to believe when Dr. Victor Sartor of Edmonton reported the facts to me on the examination table at the Royal Alexander Hospital.

Having undergone frequent compulsory examinations, including electrocardiograms, with no hint of trouble, I guess I had come to believe, "It can't happen to me." I woke up that morning in July, 1972, feeling sick. I telephoned my doctor who, after I had described the symptoms, ordered me to get down at once to the hospital. In a matter of minutes my life underwent a dramatic change, for losing the right to fly is like losing a limb or being deprived of one of your major faculties. My life was tied around my ability to move a heavier-than-air machine with skill and safety through a hostile, unnatural environment. And suddenly I was deprived of the use of that ability.

My earnest advice to young pilots, the result of my own experience, is to purchase loss-of-licence insurance while they can. It is much better to enter convalescence with a cheque for 50,000 or more with which to make a new start in life than to face a suddenly forbidding future as I, and possibly many others, have done, with very little put aside against such a contingency. Pilots make good money, but as does everyone else, they live up to their incomes.

People in all walks of life have heart attacks and I never expected any sympathy for an experience that is all too common today. What I would like to point out is that in many cases the victims recover and are able to resume their role as wage earners in a position they have established over a period of years, returning to be useful members of the business, industrial or professional world in which they move.

Such is not the luck of a pilot who depends on a fully-functioning heart as much as on good vision and good judgment. If his heart goes, all the rest avails him nothing.

Part of the therapy for any heart attack victim is to regain a feeling of being a useful, productive member of society.

I think I have achieved that, finally, by finding a new life as a charter boat operator.

I had always loved the water and admired those who move upon it to find their livelihood. They have in them much of the spirit and independence of the flier. I like to be master in my realm. As an aircraft pilot I had that feeling of being in command of my own destiny, the master of my fate, in a way, and nothing I had tried outside of flying had offered that until I went to sea.

Having decided to get a boat I spent a year trying to obtain something that I could afford and that would meet my standards. It was a difficult task for I didn't have enough money and boats are expensive. Ingeborg and I looked far and near, and considered many ideas. Luckily, in the end I found a sympathetic bank manager who made it possible for me to realize my dream.

In May of 1976 I became the skipper of a new, well-equipped, comfortable vessel, speed about 30 knots, range up to 300 miles, a self-contained, seaworthy, weatherworthy craft that thrilled the two of us and still does every time we look at it.

For the summer of my first year I worked for three months on fisheries patrol on the B.C. coast for the Federal

Department of Fisheries, beating up and down a 55-mile stretch of water north of Bella Bella. It was a novel experience being a sort of sea policeman, responsible for checking commercial and sports fishermen as to their salmon catch, making sure there was no intrusion by foreigners and that the rules were obeyed.

My airforce experience has helped in navigation and in gauging the weather. In the recreation and tourist fishing field the weather, of course, is everything. Working for the fisheries it meant less for we went every day with few exceptions. And those waters between the mainland and the outer islands like the Queen Charlottes can whip up a gale. And how it rained. I only had the canvas cover off the bridge for two days in the whole season.

It's a great place for commercial fishing, I suspect. I know of one fisherman who came home three weeks ahead of the seasonal closure after having harvested a better than $70,000 catch. Some fishermen complained it wasn't a very good year but I suspect they're like Canadian farmers who always have a grumble but seem to do very well for themselves when they add it up.

Friends have suggested that I ought to get a fish boat. My answer is "no thanks". I have every respect for those fishermen but they work hard in dangerous seas for their money and I have no wish at all to go into competition with them.

What I expect to be doing is operating my excellently equipped craft—she sleeps five and is self-contained for lengthy runs at sea—for sight-seeing and fishing parties. Those three months with the fisheries have given me an insight into the possibilities of the beautiful coastal waters of B.C. and some idea of the problems that must be dealt with by anyone who operates a sizeable boat in the strong-willed Pacific.

I really believe I have found a new niche in life, one that will in large measure meet the yearnings taught me by my first love—flying.

DIRECTION
OF TORQUE

CYCLIC CONTROL STICK ——————
THROTTLE ——————
COLLECTIVE PITCH STICK ——————
PEDALS ——————